Cover Designed by Travis E. Hills, Sr.

Published by: **Self-Published**
Printed in the United States of America
In keeping with biblical principles of creation stewardship, The Publishing Company advocates the responsible use of our natural resources. As a member of the Green Press Initiative, our company uses recycled paper when possible. The text paper of this book is comprised of 30% post-consumer waste.

Green Press INITIATIVE

Library of Congress Cataloging-in-Publication Data

Hills, Travis, 1969-
Revival of the Seven: Positioning God's People to be Blessed and Kept in Perilous Times / Travis E. Hills, Sr.
Summary: "Christian Author, Travis E. Hills, Sr. provides Biblically-Based concepts and instructions pertaining to Christian lifestyle and Church development. Travis is an experienced Design-Builder, Planner and Land Development Consultant from the construction and development industry. This message is primarily geared toward leaders within the Church, with emphasis on the sustainability within the Christian community in America as our country faces continued economic hardships into the foreseeable future."

ISBN 978-0-615-54371-0

Dedication

This book is dedicated to my dear wife, Jacqueline,
my grandmother Comina, my parents, Tommy and Gwen,
and the rest of my family who have always loved,
supported, and encouraged me throughout the years.
With much love, I am forever grateful.
May God always meet your needs.

To my children, whose generation is most impacted
by the subject matter of this book.
May you always seek to have a personal relationship with God.
May your faith and hope always be based on the
Word of God and sound doctrine.
May you come to trust in Christ Jesus for all things.

[page left blank]

Travis E. Hills, Sr.

REVIVAL OF THE SEVEN

PART – I

RESTORATION OF THE CHURCH COMMUNITY THROUGH UNITY

THE FALL OF A CHRISTIAN NATION AND THE RISE OF GLOBALIZATION

RE-INTRODUCTION TO CHURCH RESOURCE MANAGEMENT

(ACTS 6:1-8)

SUSTAINABLE LIVING FOR THE MODERN CHRISTIAN COMMUNITY

UNITED STOREHOUSE INTERNATIONAL

ONE CULTURE ~ ONE VOICE ~ ONE CHURCH

THE FIRST CENTURY CHURCH MOVEMENT

PART – I

CONTENTS

INTRODUCTION

THE PURPOSE

This book is written primarily as a message to leaders within the Church and all who consider themselves to be Christians, secondarily to everyone that needs to be rescued from the seemingly hopeless circumstances of life in a fallen world, and lastly to the world as a testimony to the goodness of God and His will for all mankind.

For the purpose of this endeavor, my definition of the Church is: any fellowship of those who believe that....

1. There is one God composed of three persons, God the Father, God the Son, and the God the Holy Spirit referred to as the Trinity or Godhead.
2. Jesus Christ is the only begotten Son of God, who was born of a virgin and dwelt among us as fully man but yet remained fully God.
3. Jesus came down from heaven to present himself as a living sacrifice for the forgiveness of sin for all mankind. Thereby, making the gift of salvation and eternal life with God in Heaven available to all who accept Him as their Lord and Savior.
4. Jesus was crucified, died, and rose from the dead on the third day.
5. The resurrected Jesus dwelt among the Apostles and ascended into heaven and is seated at the right hand of God the father.
6. When Jesus ascended into Heaven, the Holy Spirit came to comfort, empower and dwell among His people until Christ returns.
7. Jesus is coming back for His bride, the Church, at an exact moment which only God the Father knows.

These are the fundamental proclamations made by Jesus with regards to His deity, His identity, His purpose and His mission as found in the Gospels. Regardless of doctrine, denomination, order of service or style of worship, if you believe in these things and are connected to a body of like-minded believers, you are a part of the Church as God has made no distinction between His people.

[2nd Acts 15:8-9]

If you believe these things and desire to connect with other believers but haven't found a Church that is suitable for meeting your spiritual needs, this book is a message for you that will inspire you to get connected to partake in the next big move of God for the Church.

If you are not a believer in these things but you recognize the need for being rescued from the hopelessness of life in this fallen world, this book will introduce you to the people that God has commissioned to lead you to salvation through Christ Jesus.

If you are just curious about Christian lifestyle, this book will guide you to the source that instructs all Christians on how to live and provide you with an opportunity to consider the lifestyle that God desires for you. The USI project is designed to encourage the Church and its leadership to examine itself in a "relative" sense with consideration toward differences between the cultures and societies that impacted the first century Christians in comparison to the modern Church.

POINT OF VIEW

This book is intended to provide a "brief", yet "broad", overview of events and actions that have led to the current conditions and hardships being faced by average Christian families in America today.

Statistics are used to establish standards and draw distinctions and comparisons between what was, what is and what is being suggested or proposed to come.

Historical References are used to create a frame of reference and background for readers that may not be informed about these facts and events. Furthermore, this text seeks to share a perspective that suggests that there has been a continuum, particularly over the past few decades, that leads to an intended end result, which happens to be in-line with Bible prophecy.

Program Concepts are excerpts from a strategic plan developed for the modern Church. These concepts are proposed as viable solutions toward addressing the problems noted in an organized, uniformed and systematic manner with a "corporate approach" through a project referred to as United Storehouse International (USI).

There are a number of ideals suggested and concepts proposed which may be considered by some as speculative in nature within this book. However, this content is based on principles and prophecies found in the Holy Bible. The ideals shared within this book are at least equivalent to the vast range of speculation being provided by the world's leading social scientists, political analysts and economists regarding the current state of our culture and economy with regards to forecasting what the future may bring. The USI concept offers a practical and comprehensive approach to dealing with the conditions and hardships being faced by today's average Christian family in America, aside from the belief that this message is inspired by the Holy Spirit through His Word.

This book seeks to provide a **biblically-based point of view** that shapes the reader's perspective toward serving the needs of the Church, its members and those who seek a more rewarding and fulfilling existence in life that extends to eternity with God.

THE BIG PICTURE PERSPECTIVE

As followers of Christ, we believe what the word of God says regarding the "Big Picture" of life on earth. We know that God is the sovereign creator of the universe and all that is within it.

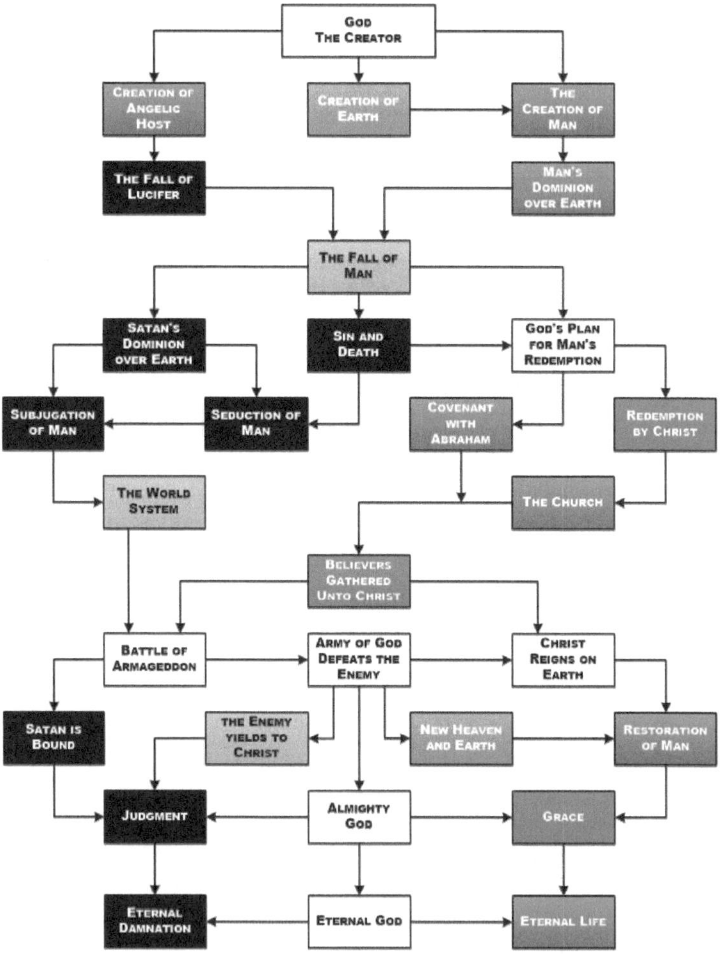

1. *Creation of Heaven and Earth*
2. *Fall of Lucifer from Heaven*
3. *Fall of man from Fellowship with God*
4. *Satan gains dominion over the Earth*
5. *Covenant between God and Israel through Abraham*
6. *Redemption of mankind through Jesus Christ*
7. *Covenant between God and the Church through Jesus Christ*
8. *Union of Christ and His People*
9. *Satan is defeated*
10. *Restoration of man through the Kingdom of God on Earth*
11. *Damnation of Satan and Judgment of the World*
12. *Eternity with God*

ACT ONE: CREATION AND THE FALL

God created the Angels as servants to His will in Heaven and Earth. Lucifer, the Arc Angel, fell from grace and was cast down from Heaven to the Earth. The Earth was formed in 6 days. Man was created and placed in an anointed garden called Eden where the spirit of God dwelt. Man was given dominion over the Earth and everything within it. Man was engaged by the fallen angel Lucifer (now called Satan) in the form of a serpent and coerced to disobey God. Man was introduced to Sin and death as a result of his disobedience.

ACT TWO: REDEMPTION OF MAN

God found pleasure in the ways of His servant Abram and established a covenant with him, changing his name to Abraham, meaning "father of many nations". God promised Abraham that his descendants would be God's chosen people and as numerous as the stars. Jesus, the only begotten son of God, was born of a virgin who was a descendent of Abraham. Jesus was born to redeem mankind from sin by being the perfect and final blood sacrifice. Jesus was crucified, died, and rose from the dead on the third day in accordance with prophecy. As a result, all who believe in the risen messiah and accept His sacrifice for our sins are redeemed in the eyes of God.

ACT THREE: RESTORATION OF MAN

Jesus Christ promised that He would return to earth to claim His bride, the Church. Upon His return, He will vanquish the enemy and establish His kingdom on earth in Jerusalem. Man shall be restored to his original form as it was in the Garden of Eden. Dominion shall be returned to man under the authority of Jesus Christ.

In light of these facts, we should live our daily lives in accordance with the knowledge of how things ultimately work out. The war against the enemy, Satan and his army, the world system, is already won by the army of the Lord. Our short time on Earth is designed to be spent in preparation for our lives in Eternity.

CHAPTER I

CRITICAL CHOICES IN CRITICAL TIMES

SYSTEMS OF CAESAR AND OF GOD

As we grow closer to the time of Christ's return, delineation between the paths of life and death are becoming blatantly clear. Ironically, Jesus said that choosing the path of eternal life will come at the cost of experiencing the death of our flesh. We have entered a period of time when Christians can't afford to choose the wrong socio-economic path. There will be no way back to the opportunity of choice. How we choose to invest our resources today will dictate the path that we will ultimately end up traveling.

DEFINING SUCCESS, ACHIEVEMENT AND PROSPERITY

DREAMERS AND DREAM MAKERS

Prosperity in America has been defined by the accumulation of material things and the degree of access to indulgences. Capitalism works on the premise of winners and losers with the participants being dreamers (consumers) and dream makers (manufacturers).

The dream making process includes:

- Manufacturing: Manufactures the dream
- Banking: Finances the dream
- Services: Delivers, Maintains and Repairs the dream
- Multi-Media: Promotes and Supports the dream
- Marketing: Sells the dream
- Government: Regulates the dream

The dream making industry is primarily controlled by people within the ruling socio-economic class. Their primary objective is to convince the public that what they are offering is what everyone should want and must have in order to live a fulfilling life. They use vital base ingredients combined with lots of additives to strengthen the attraction to the product.

For example, flavored soft drinks use the vital base ingredient of water, which is an absolute human necessity. However, the soft drink industry depends on the emotional desire to experience flavor and choice. Manufacturers ensure their continued success through adding ingredients that inherently cause cravings or addictions.

Another example is automobile sales. Effective means of transportation have always been a necessity from the beginning of mankind. However, automobile makers depend on the emotional desire to make transportation a personal reflection of their character and social status. Therefore, suggestive marketing influences the popular culture of consumers. Manufacturers fulfill their desires with products and services while bankers make acquisition possible by providing affordable financing.

They make it seem as if everyone is involved but you so that you are inclined to join in. The dream makers have substantially achieved their goals by erasing the line between wants and needs for the majority of the American public, with emphasis on women and children. Manufacturers have also promoted an attitude or state of mind toward the pursuit of dreams in order to keep the attention of the consumer focused on the products and services being offered. The world simply employs tactics through media that exploit the nature of human beings, such as; pride, greed, envy and jealousy with emphasis on "entitlement". Constant evoking of these emotions creates a strong desire for appeasement and ensures a constant pursuit of self-satisfaction through consumption rather than contentment. The consumer's primary objective is to fulfill their dreams.

The basic Christian lifestyle works on the assurance of the blessed hope in eternal salvation for the saved and hopelessness for the lost. Personal contentment is at the core of the culture which brings about feelings of humility and gratitude.

DESIRE TO WIN

The concept of winning in America is strongly supported by identifying specific traits and practices to classify as losing. There are no winners in capitalism without producing losers in the process. Over the years, people have allowed popular culture to define what is considered to be a winning posture instead of traditional values. Examples of what is considered to be a winning posture for a typical Capitalist Consumer include things such as:

- Owning a home in a prestigious community
- Earning high wages (like entertainers and athletes)
- Driving an late-modeled or expensive car
- Wearing the latest fashions
- Using name-brand products

Examples of a Capitalist losing posture have included:

- Renting a home in an average community
- Earning low wages
- Wearing used clothing
- Using generic products

The media portrays a society where most people appear to be winning and everyone has a chance to become a winner even though statistics will prove that less than 1/3 of the population are able to comfortably partake in this lifestyle in a fiscally responsible manner. Capitalism keeps the focus on winning so that the majority of people are always in pursuit of being counted as a winner according to the world's standards.

Winning is defined for Christians by Jesus Christ and the Apostle Paul as being those who endure hardship and persecution for the sake of the Gospel. Losing is to give in to the allurement of the world and become a part of its system.

THE WORLD'S SYSTEM

This system is driven by man's promotion of himself being self-sufficient without need of God. This mentality is influenced by Satan casting a spirit of darkness over those who are yielded to the pride of life and the love of pleasure.

Examples:

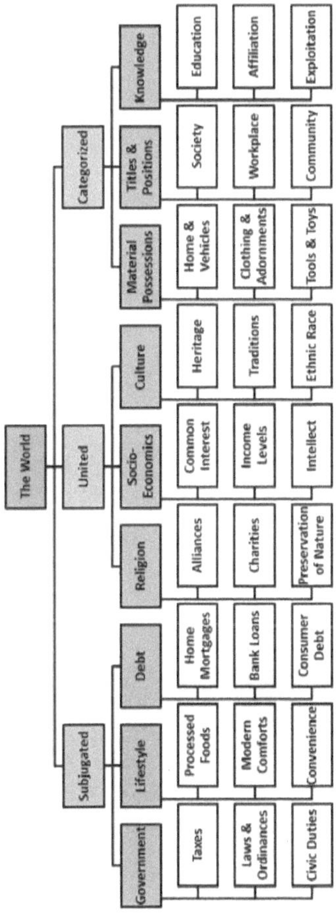

THE CHURCH'S SYSTEM

This system is guided by man's submission to the authority of Jesus Christ and acknowledgement of his need for salvation. This mindset is a result of the Holy Spirit dwelling within those who are yielded to the Will of God and accountable to His Word.

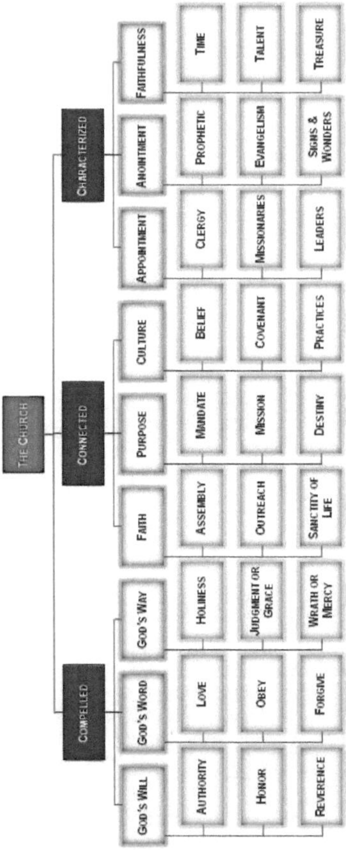

BEING IN THE RACE: PARTICIPANTS, FINISHERS & WINNERS

Many people have desired to run in a marathon. To take part in a marathon, one must commit to a time of training. This time would typically include mental and physical exercises along with changes in one's lifestyle regiment in order to increase the chances of success. Everyone that registers for the race does so with the intention of completing the course. However, there are many different motivating factors that drive individual participants.

- Some will participate because they were challenged by others.
- Some will participate as a test of endurance to themselves.
- Some will participate to increase their stamina and ability to compete
- Some will participate to compete and win

Though there are several types of participants with a multitude of varying motivating factors, they all share a common desire to participate in the same event and reach a relative form of success. The accomplishments will range from those who begin the race and are unable to complete it to those who complete the race well. There will undoubtedly be a winner of the race that will be recognized and rewarded accordingly. However, there will be those that overcome great disadvantages and adversity who go on to complete the race against the odds. They shall be admired and celebrated for their accomplishment. Last, but not least, there will be those who tried and failed to reach the finish line. They shall be recognized for their efforts and their will to participate. Regardless of placement, all participants will be acknowledged and invited to partake in the celebration and festivities following the event.

Life has often been compared to running in a race. The world is focused on winners and losers. In America, we refer to our system of capitalism as a rat-race, which implies that we are like rodents that will do anything to survive. Winning this race ultimately dictates that only the strong will survive and the weak shall perish.

The Christian life puts emphasis on enduring until the end rather than placing first. In fact, Jesus said that those who finish first in this life shall be last and those who finish last shall be first in the Kingdom of Heaven. Jesus also said that the meek shall inherit the earth. *[Matthew 5:5]* Therefore, those who are considered as weak by the world (for the sake of Christ) shall ultimately be victorious through the power of the Holy Spirit.

Recognition of these vastly different paths has become as clear to see as any time in human history. However, choosing the path of righteousness has never been more difficult as the Church has been systematically drawn into the world system over time. Our participation in one of these races is the evidence of our choice before God and man. *[1 Peter 4:1-19]*

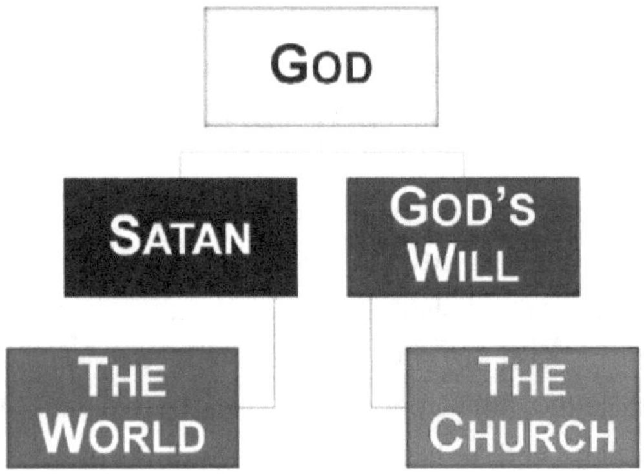

CHAPTER II

CARETAKERS OF THE CHURCH

MEETING THE NEEDS WITHIN THE CHURCH

The early believers understood that as a result of their conversion, it became necessary for them to band together. They realized that this faith required unity among them. They actively sought to establish "complete" commonality of lifestyle as they served a common Lord. They shared their wealth, their homes, their food, their burdens and their faith with one another.

[Acts 2:42-47]

As the number of followers continually grew, so did the need for oversight and leadership of the newly-formed Church and its members. Peter was approached by members of the Church concerning unjust treatment to some of its members. In this particular case, it was the widows of a particular Christian community.

Peter was not compelled to become involved in such matters as he was focused on the prime directive of spreading the Gospel. However, he recognized the need for taking care of the people's physical needs along with the spiritual, as Jesus always did. Peter responded to the situation by calling a meeting with the other Apostles along with all of the disciples to choose seven men who were known to be "Spirit-filled" and "wise" from among them to become the administrators of the Church. They would be fully responsible for making sure that the members were being attended to.

CHOOSING SEVEN CARETAKERS OF THE CHURCH

As in the days of the early (Apostolic) Church, the needs of the members have grown beyond its ability to address in an equitable and uniformed way. The leaders of the Church are faced with addressing the needs in the same way that the Apostles did. It would not be right for the ministers of the Gospel to stop what they are doing and serve those who have already received the gift of salvation. However, it remains critically important that the physical needs of the God's people be attended to along with the spiritual so that they are not drawn to the world in search of fulfillment.

There are few specific accounts in the Bible regarding what the seven leaders actually did to accomplish the task of looking after the Church members or how they did it. We can assume that they did not simply go about solving daily problems, like providing food and clothing for those in need with miracles, as Jesus frequently did throughout His ministry on earth. These men must have taken a strategic approach to carrying out their responsibilities successfully. The first century Church increased exponentially, often adding thousands of new members in a day.

[Acts 2:41]

There must have been a system used to govern membership entitlements and equitable distribution. There must have been levels of management and cell groups or congregations established to make the ratios between servers and recipients manageable. Lower-level leaders must have been recruited and trained to manage Church business at each level. I believe that the original seven were uniquely talented and highly skilled in addition to their known anointing and gifts of wisdom and knowledge.

[Acts 6:1-7]

These men must have had insight and skills in many areas, including:

1. Planning / Preparation
2. Program Development
3. Protocol Development
4. Project Management
5. Accounting / Bookkeeping
6. Risk Management
7. Human Resource Management

We might assume that their God-led efforts played a significant supporting role in the establishing the foundation for the institutional aspect of the Apostolic Church.

UNITED WE STAND

This message urges the Church to lead by example in responding to the needs of its people in these most difficult times. The information within this book is an introduction to a concept / program that is being presented through the United Storehouse International (USI) project. Many Churches and Christian organizations may already have similar programs in place that are designed to meet the needs of its congregation and local community. I commend those groups and seek to establish or improve "connectivity" between those who are on the leading edge of Church development and stewardship along with those who need or desire improvement in those areas of their ministry.

This endeavor is "specifically" geared toward "in-reach" to the Church's membership. The USI project is not designed to augment or make suggestions toward "outreach" activities within the Church.

USI is "not focused" on the "delineation of doctrines" between denominations within the Church.

The USI project is "focused" on, and geared toward, the fortification of Church infrastructure through encouraging and developing "tangible" platforms of "commonality" that connect all Christians through revisiting and emulating relevant aspects from the structure of the first century Church.

The program seeks to re-engage issues like caring for "Widows and Orphans" along with the potential of expanding these designations in accordance with current realities of the "circumstantially needy" in today's modern Church. Hence, responding to their needs as we are instructed to by the word of God. The USI project advocates the "Revival of the Seven" Deacon Elders chosen by a council of the

Apostles and disciples, as directed by Peter, to be responsible for meeting the needs of the people within the Church.

[Acts 6:1-7]

This message is not one of condemnation, but to the contrary, one of affirmation, praise and recognition of the great work that has gone forth from, and within, the Church in modern times and continues to this very day.

CHURCH DENOMINATIONS: DIVERSITY WITHOUT DIVISION

I believe that major divisions and denominations of the one Church can be likened unto the Trinity and attributes of God. The Trinity (Father, Son and Holy Spirit) represent the functional divisions of the One God often referred to as the "Godhead." Each part of the Trinity has distinction toward carrying out the will of God. His attributes are as numerous as His relation to all things in creation.

A few of God's major attributes in relation to His people are:

1. Eternal God: He who always was is and forever shall be.
2. Holy God: He who is perfect, blameless and set-aside.
3. All-Powerful God: He who controls and dominates the universe.
4. Omni-Present God: He who is always present in all places at all times.
5. All-Knowing God: He who knows all that was, all that is and all that shall be.
6. Sovereign God: He who is the one true and living God.
7. Jealous God: He who desires worship, praise and honor from all of His creations.
8. Loving God: He who is the embodiment of love and the essence of its meaning.
9. Gracious God: He who forgives and blesses the undeserving.

10. Merciful God: He who shows mercy to all that seek salvation through Christ.

I believe that the "One Church" can reflect varying attributes of God's word expressed through diverse perspectives, experiences and relationships between God and man without division.

DIVIDE AND CONQUER

There are literally thousands of denominations within the Church. The vast majority of these denominations originated in the U.S. resulting from the government's freedom of religion policy, which founded this nation. The vast number of Christian denominations is only possible when governments are either in partnership with the Church or tolerant of Christians. These conditions promote the atmosphere that supports freedom of religion. Anytime that mankind has been given the opportunity to choose, his fallen nature tends to move away from God's plan instead of closer to Him. Only when being faced with calamity and persecution does mankind look toward God and become open to His plan.

We are living in an age when governments are breaking their ties with the Church and Christianity. In contrast, the process of globalization supports tolerance of immorality and pluralism (acknowledgement of many gods). The core principles of the original Apostolic Church and its effectiveness in the world will not continue without unification of the Church for as Jesus said, a house divided against itself cannot stand. The Apostle Paul also appealed for agreement and unity within the Church.

[Matthew 12:25, 1 Corinthians 1:10, Ephesians 4:11-13]

Other world religions are seeking to galvanize their constituencies into a unified global force as evidenced in the middle-east and northern Africa being predominantly Islamic. The lie of self-preservation has been planted within the American Church. The notion of this concept has permeated the belief system of many

Christian denominations, especially those who subscribe to the separatist movement. Survivalist and many conservative voices within the Church are saying "save yourselves" instead of promoting strategic efforts to "preserve the body." Ironically, the Bible teaches us that the more we try to insulate ourselves from harm the more vulnerable we become. Jesus said that only when we seek to save others for the sake of Christ shall we ultimately be saved, even though this is a "counter-intuitive" response to adversity for most people.

[Matthew 13:25-26, Mark 8:35]

Many have become obsessed with obtaining silver and gold in the attempt to secure their personal wealth. This can easily be used as a deception tactic to further isolate believers within the body of Christ. The enemy will seek to rob wealthy Christians of their assets as an assault to their faith. People who have invested heavily into their personal assets will be consumed with protecting their wealth when calamity strikes. There will be safety in the body for all who invest their assets into the storehouse. God will faithfully provide for His people, supply all of their needs and sustain them through perilous times, as He has always done, by their faith and obedience to His word and His will.

[Proverbs 27:19-20, Acts 3:6-7, Luke:12-32-34]

TIME FOR THE CHURCH TO BE PREPARED AND ON GUARD

In the times of great distress that are forthcoming, many Churches will not be prepared. In the days leading up to these times, many weak-spirited and unfaithful pastors, Church leaders and laity alike, will be blinded by denial and complacency. They will fail to recognize or accept the magnitude of calamity that is soon to come.

When confronted they will say things like:

- "Our leaders must be aware of these things and they wouldn't let anything like that happen without being prepared or at least warning us in advance"

- "I believe that we still have time because they've been saying that the end was coming for years and they were always wrong"
- "I'm more of an optimist and I believe that things will work out in the long run and get back to normal"
- "I have faith that God wouldn't let anything bad happen to me regardless of what's going on in the world around me"
- "We've been through tough times before and somehow we always manage to get through it"
- "I believe that if anyone is going to survive this threat that I will be one of them"
- "There is nothing that we can do but pray and hope for God to come soon"

They will ignore the instructions, warnings and admonitions of the scriptures concerning the return of Christ and the responsibilities of believers as we await His coming. They will seek alignment with the world rather than separation from its perverse and wicked ways.

[Matthew 24:10-11]

They will use the resources of their congregations to maintain a "status quo" environment that is compatible with the world around them. They will continue to focus on outreach and giving while their members suffer in silence lest they are singled-out and made to feel inadequate among the congregation. Pastors will make plans for a future of prosperity without having recognized that there has been a change of season to a time of preparation for a season of sorrows.

[Luke 12:54-56, 1 Thessalonians 5: 1-11]

They will find agreement with the world's demands that Israel be further marginalized through giving up its homeland to those who would call for their destruction. They will be given over to their own deception and become subject to demonic influence and the rule of mankind.

[Luke 21:20]

WARNING OF PERILOUS DAYS AHEAD

1 Peter 4:1-19

Then suddenly, catastrophic events and devastation will come from within the earth accompanied by global economic collapse. Chaos will quickly engulf civil society and life as we know it will forever be changed. Many believers and non-believers will go to their local Churches seeking refuge and relief from the extreme adversity of conditions. Many Churches will quickly become overwhelmed as they have not prepared to respond in a time of emergency nor have they made adequate provisions for their very own members. Many pastors and Church leaders will pray for relief but their prayers will not be answered for the time will have come when no man can work and must rely on the yield of whatever actions have been taken prior to this time (as in the parable of the wise and foolish bridesmaids). *[Matthew 25:1]*

These Churches will not survive and will be abandoned by its members. In desperation, many of the unfaithful Church goers will seek refuge offered by the world for survival. They will be forced to comply with the demands of the unified government system which will place their souls in jeopardy of damnation. Many soul-winning gains that had been claimed by the Church will be "quickly diminished" as a result of the Church's complacency.

[Matthew 3:10, Matthew 7:24-27]

As for the Churches that took heed to the signs and made preparations for the time of emergency, they will assemble according to their plan. There will be little to no provisions for those who did not partake in the Church's preparation. As it was in the days of Noah, the people were warned but did not respond until it was too late.

However, faithful Churches will have set aside provisions to help some, as directed by the Holy Spirit. After the initial trauma of these events subsides, the surviving Churches will be in a position to provide leadership to their communities while helping to meet their needs. God will show favor to His people as they faithfully endure. All of their efforts and endeavors shall be blessed and they will thrive. Many unbelievers will be led to Christ and souls will be saved as a result of the Church's obedience.

The people of the last Church shall attribute their survival to having embraced a commitment to being accountable and faithful stewards of God's provisions along with the formation of covenant bonds with each other.

[Proverbs 27:12, Proverbs 6:6-8, Matthew 18:29-30]

CHAPTER III

THE U.S. 40-YEAR TRANSFORMATION 1976 – 2016

CONTROLLED BY GOD'S TIMING

POLITICIANS: PAWNS IN GOD'S PLAN

God has used the rulers of nations to carry out His will since civilization began. From tyrants to noblemen, God has allowed them to bring curses and blessings to the people in accordance with His overarching master plan to redeem mankind. It is also part of God's master plan to bring final judgment against Lucifer, the fallen Arc angel that rebelled against God and was cast down from Heaven, along with all who have chosen to follow him.

The fundamental agendas of most politicians are to gain notoriety and power while establishing a historical legacy for themselves and their descendants. Additionally, some seek to expand their personal wealth or to exert authority and control over others. Few simply seek to serve and do what is right according to the will of God and the goodwill of the people. Regardless of their motives, God uses them all to bring about portions of His plan. In the case of the Egyptian Pharaoh in the time of Moses, his agenda was driven by the fact that the Jews had become so numerous that they posed a threat to national security in the event of war. The Jews were originally made slaves in response to this threat. Virtually any ruler, having good or bad intensions, would have responded to this situation with his own best interest, and that of his constituency, in mind. In this case, Pharaoh minimized the threat while using the Jews to further his agenda through using their slave labor for building monuments to his legacy. God allows the agendas of rulers to go forth until the time for change arrives in accordance with His master plan.

THE SEVEN DAYS OF GOD: FROM CREATION WEEK TO JUDGMENT DAY

I believe that the sincerity of the heart and prayers of God's people is pivotally tied to the way God executes His plan during times of shifting paradigms. This reality was evidenced throughout the Old Testament scriptures when the prophets called the people to repentance. God was either moved by their repentance to spare them from destruction or destroyed them for being unrepentant. This is a critical reason why Christians must take note of the times in which they live. Historically, when God's people are in danger of widespread persecution and oppression along with rampant immorality and sexual deviancy, a paradigm shift in God's plan is bound to take place.

In order to be conscious of the times we must first understand the relativity that God has placed on time and numbers. We can look back to the beginning with the creation of the earth in accordance with scriptures. God created the earth in six days and rested on the seventh day. Let us take an account of each of those days.

1. Day One: God created light and established distinction between night and day.
    - One marked ***the beginning*** of His plan
2. Day Two: God created the atmosphere and called it "sky"
    - Two set the ***general conditions*** surrounding His plan
3. Day Three: God gathered the waters of the earth and established dry ground. The waters were called "seas" and the dry ground was called "land". The land was populated with all forms of vegetation.
    - Three ***established the basis*** of His plan
4. Day Four: God created the Sun, Moon and stars to serve as greater light in the day and lesser lights at night. They would also mark the time for seasons, days and years.
    - Four ***shed light*** on His plan
5. Day Five: God created the creature of the sea and air.
    - Five brought in the ***supporting characters*** in His plan
6. Day Six: God created the land animals and last, but not least man. Man was given dominion over the earth and everything in it.

   - Six brought in the ***main characters*** in His plan

7. Day Seven: God had completed His work and rested, declaring this day as holy.
   - Seven marked the ***completed work*** of His Plan

Creation provides a glimpse of number sequences that God uses to carry out His plans on earth. Sin was released by Adam in the Garden of Eden and subdued by Jesus on the Cross at Calvary. Approximately 2,000 years passed between Adam and Abraham. Approximately 2,000 years passed between Abraham and Jesus. There have been approximately 2,000 years between Jesus and the present. This accounts for 6,000 years since the beginning with Adam. The Apostle Peter said: "with God, ***a day is like a thousand years and a thousand years is like a day***." *[2 Peter 3:8]* Therefore, let's consider what has transpired on each 1,000-year day since the beginning.

1. Day-1: 4,000-3,000 BC ***the beginning***
   - Creation Week-The Beginning
   - The fall of man
2. Day-2: 3,000-2,000 BC ***general conditions***
   - Birth & Life of Noah
   - The Flood purges the earth
3. Day-3: 2,000-1,000 BC ***established the basis***
   - Birth & Life of Abraham
     - ***The Promise of the Nation of Israel***
   - Birth & Life of Jacob
     - The 12 Tribes of Israel are formed
   - Birth & Life of Moses
     - ***The Law is Established***
   - ***Joshua Leads Israel into the promised land***
4. Day-4: 1,000 BC - Christ ***shed light***

- Rule of David
  - God's chosen King of Israel
- Birth & Life of Solomon
  - Solomon Builds the Temple of God
- Nebuchadnezzar Captures Jerusalem and Destroys the Temple that Solomon built
- The Jews are exiled and Tribes are disbanded
- ***Christ is Born***

5. Day-5: Christ-1,000 AD ***supporting characters***
   - Christ brings the Gospel of Salvation
   - Christ is Crucified, Died and Rose from the Grave
   - Christ Ascends into Heaven and the Holy Spirit comes to Empower and Comfort the Believers
   - ***Peter starts the Church***
   - ***The Apostolic Church is Unified***
6. Day-6: 1,000-2,000 AD ***main characters***
   - The Church Divides into Eastern and Western
   - Constantine leads the Crusades
   - ***Israel is Returned to the Jews and the Tribes are reunited***
   - ***The Church Re-unites in preparation for Christ's Return***
   - Christ Returns and Defeats Satan and the armies of the World at the Battle of Armageddon
7. Day-7: 2,000-3,000 AD ***completed work***
   - Christ Establishes His Kingdom in Jerusalem
   - ***Man is Renewed and Restored***
   - Christ Rules for 1,000 years (Millennial Reign)

- The Day of Judgment

GENERAL NOTE

*INFORMATION FOUND IN THIS BOOK IS **NOT** INTENDED TO BE A SOURCE FOR HISTORICAL REFERENCE. HOWEVER, HISTORICAL ACCOUNTS ARE REFERENCED FOR THE PURPOSE OF RECOUNTING EVENTS THAT PROVIDE THE READER WITH A "PERSPECTIVE" ON AMERICA'S PATH TOWARD GLOBALIZATION AND THE NEED FOR UNITY WITHIN THE CHURCH FOR SUCH A TIME AS THIS.*

FOUNDED AS A CHRISTIAN NATION

The United States of America established a constitution in its founding that promoted Life, Liberty and the Pursuit of Happiness. Freedom of speech and religion was at the forefront of these ideals. Christianity was the national religion by which the laws of this land were created. The U.S. adopted capitalism as its fundamental philosophy toward free-market economics and industry. Though the intensions of the constitution were well-meaning, one of its framers, Thomas Jefferson, one of this country's greatest leaders, warned against the consequences of our government falling into the hands of the ungodly. He wrote:

> "I sincerely wish... we could see our government so secured as to depend less on the character of the person in whose hands it is trusted. Bad men will sometimes get in and with such an immense patronage may make great progress in corrupting the public mind and principles. This is a subject with which wisdom and patriotism should be occupied."
>
> [Thomas Jefferson to Moses Robinson, 1801].

TWO HUNDRED YEARS IN THE MAKING

July 4, 1776 marks our nation's declaration of independence from British rule. From the 1770's to the 1970's (1776-1976), America grew and prospered under the guides of being known as a Christian Nation for 200 years. During the same timeframe, a secret society organization known as the Illuminati was established and thrived. The Illuminati is an occult (secret) group formed from a combination of Free Masonry and Rosicrucianism. Founded on May 1, 1776 by Adam Weishaupt, this group has set its goals on establishing a New World Order by achieving the following stated objectives:

1. Abolition of all ordered governments
2. Abolition of private property
3. Abolition of inheritance
4. Abolition of patriotism
5. Abolition of the family
6. Abolition of religion
7. Creation of a world government

Their means and methods are primarily implemented through subversive acts and conspiracies at the highest levels of our society designed to gain control of government, media, and the monetary system. The Illuminati's membership and influence has proliferated throughout all areas of government, media, and private industry across the United States and around the world.

Many milestone events took place in the 1970's that set the stage for globalization and the secularization of America. The leaders of this great nation have chosen to place the agendas of mankind ahead of its founding commitment to God just as the children of Israel did. America has embarked on a forty-year journey to globalization through the wilderness of this post-Christian U.S. society.

FROM NATIONAL SOVEREIGNTY TO GLOBAL INTERDEPENDENCE

ECONOMIC

- Actions
  - Creation of Free Trade Zones
  - Increased Foreign Trade and Government Spending Debts
  - Increased Dependence on Foreign Oil
  - Reduction of Trade Tariffs
  - Decreased Control of Capital Flow
  - Increased Subsidies for Global Companies
  - Creation of Global Patent and Copyright Laws
  - Reduction of International Shipping Cost
- Results
  - Decreased value of Currency
  - Decreased Average Household Wealth
  - Increased Dependence on Foreign Labor
  - Reduction of Domestic Corporate Incentives
  - Decrease in Domestic Industry and Job Availability
  - Increased U.S. Household Dependency on Government Aid

CULTURAL

- Actions
  - Elimination of Christianity as National Religion
  - Reduction of Privacy Rights
  - Restrictions to Freedom of Speech
  - Reduction of Liberal Arts Educational Requirements
  - Increased Computer-Based Electronics
  - Decreased Emphasis on Reading and Outdoor Activities
  - Increased Dependence on Processed Foods
  - Decreased Emphasis on Natural Healthy Lifestyle

- Results
  - Decreased Moral and Ethical Values
  - Loss of Freedom and Civil Liberties
  - Decreased Quality of Public Education
  - Increased Dependence on the Internet
  - Increased Dependence on Electronic Media and Entertainment
  - Increased Dependence on Prescription Drugs
  - Increased Need for Government Healthcare

SECULARIZATION

THE "BOOMER" GENERATION

America was considered to be the most powerful nation on Earth after World War II. War veterans returning to the U.S. reunited with their wives. Many unmarried veterans quickly got married to women that they became intimately involved with in deference to the moral standards of the prevailing Christian society. As a result, the U.S. experienced a population explosion known as "the baby boom." The generation of children born during this post-WWII period was commonly referred to as "Boomers." Abroad, the American government focused on communist aggression, particularly in Russia and south-east Asia.

The U.S. was committed to preventing the spread of communism throughout the region, which led to the Korean War and ultimately the war in Viet-Nam. This war was unpopular with U.S. citizens. Many Americans believed that the U.S. military was being wrongfully used for political gain at the expense of U.S. soldiers and the Vietnamese people.

THE U.S. COUNTERCULTURE REVOLUTION:

The children of the Boomer generation, (commonly referred to as Generation "X" or the 13th Generation) had been raised in the relative peace and prosperity that followed after World War II. While soldiers fought and died in the jungles of Viet-Nam, millions of Americans, primarily led by college students, were in protest of the war back at home. This generation of U.S. citizens had not experienced the carnage of major wars or the adversities associated with economic collapse. They did not perceive that their personal freedom was at-risk from foreign aggressors nor did they accept the historical fact that peace could only be achieved or maintained by use of force.

They were raised with the notion that America fought and won a war to protect their constitutional rights to life, liberty and the pursuit of happiness. As a result, they became obsessed with protecting all forms of life, experiencing all forms of liberty and the pursuit of happiness. These post-war conditions gave way to the rise of a countercultural group that called themselves the "Beat" generation (or Beatniks), which ultimately merged into the Hippie movement. They developed a concept of freedom based on ideals like "free-love" through sexual promiscuity and "unity" through communal living, which was in stark contrast to the traditional values of this Judeo-Christian nation and the original intent of the U.S. Constitution. The Hippie movement advocated peace at all cost. "Make love not war" was the slogan coined that became a symbolic characterization of this generation. Widespread illicit drug use was also commonly associated with this generation. Marijuana and Psychedelic drugs like LSD were most popular and readily accessible.

THE ADVANCEMENT OF COUNTERCULTURAL MOVEMENTS

The social environment produced by the Beatnik and Hippie generation promoted the formulation of many special interest groups that formed non-profit organizations and movements that gave voice to the rights of any group of people that shared a common belief. These movements spanned the gambit from animal rights to human rights, from the right to bear arms to the right to smoke marijuana.

Countercultural groups eventually developed a unified political viewpoint that ultimately took on the meaning liberalism in America. Those who subscribed to these political viewpoints became known as "Liberals" based on the philosophy that the will of the majority should rule over the structure government. The Liberals political rivals and nemesis became known as "Conservatives", who generally believed that traditional moral values, based in Judeo-Christianity, should prevail within the structure of government for the sake of the republic, even if it is not the will of the majority.

The Liberals dominated the Democratic Party and the Conservatives controlled the Republican Party. The Liberals waged political warfare against the Conservatives and the U.S. government establishment in the courts by seeking to place allies in the congress and on the U.S. Supreme Court. Many private businesses benefited by supporting Liberal agendas, especially broadcast media and manufacturers of consumer products. This era also gave birth to a number of new "well-financed" and powerful organizations designed solely to support political views and agendas referred to as Political Action Committees (or PACs). Great moral battles were won, such as the civil rights laws of the late 1960's. Great moral defeats took place as in the case of Roe vs. Wade in 1973 which legalized abortion in America.

MODERN TECHNOLOGY ADVANCES BY QUANTUM LEAPS

In the aftermath of WWII, scientist and engineers remained focused on expanding new technologies created during the war. By the 1970's, many pivotal technologies were emerging from college campuses and government laboratories into the mainstream marketplace. The atmosphere of freedom inspired by the Boomer generation led to quantum leaps in expanding technology and innovation from the U.S.

There were a number of milestones in technology that took place in the 1970's, such as:

- Microwave Ovens become accessible to average U.S. households
- ARPANET (predecessor to the internet) is born
- Intel introduces the first microprocessor
- MITS introduces Altair 8800 the first personal computer
- Microsoft was born
- Apple Computers was born

- NASA unveils the first Space Shuttle named Enterprise
- Home video recorder/players were made public
- The Internet concept was developed
- The first commercially viable arcade and home video games were made and Atari was born

THE TURNING POINT - AMERICAN VULNERABILITY IS REVEALED

America's eventual "abrupt" withdrawal from the Viet-Nam war was a milestone event in American History. The withdrawal without defeating the enemy exposed vulnerability in the U.S. and its ability to force its will on a sovereign nation. The world took note to the fact that guerilla warfare tactics, involving various forms of terrorism were used effectively against the U.S.

Women and children were often used as suicide bombers or human shields against U.S. soldiers in combat. The enemy often embedded themselves in civilian villages. Though the opposing force suffered heavy casualties, they never surrendered. Some viewed this as a defeat to the American military, even more devastating, a defeat to the spread of American democracy.

SOCIETAL STANDARDS FOR U.S. FAMILIES

Living in the U.S. comes with a number of societal standards that are "heavily" promoted by private industry, the media and supported by our government, being a free-market capitalistic society. America is no longer a Christian nation having societal and community standards that are primarily influenced by the Bible. Virtually all societal and community standards in the U.S. are set by private industry through multi-media inundation. American standards are derived from an exploitive interpretation of our "so-called" inalienable rights to Life, Liberty and the Pursuit of Happiness.

Based on 20th century Supreme Court decisions, life is no longer an inalienable right for all Americans, particularly the unborn. Liberty is constantly being eroded by censorship, freedom of speech restrictions and receding right to privacy laws. In the age of digital information, live "uncensored" broadcast is virtually a thing of the past. Digital technology provides the ability for images to be delayed and censored "at-will" by government regulatory agencies. All forms of electronic media are moving toward being digital. All that remains is the pursuit of happiness. It seems that this pursuit is intentionally being made "increasingly" more elusive to keep us "perpetually" interested in buying something new. The pursuit of happiness is the "lifeblood" of capitalism. By contrast, contentment is its enemy.

[Romans 12:3-21, 13:12-14, 1 Thessalonians 4:9-12, Philippians 4:11-13]

ACCESS TO MULTI-MEDIA

In the early 1980's, print media, fm radio, and major television networks still dominated the media with a growing challenge from cable television. The internet and satellite radio were in their infancy. By the 90's, cable television rivaled network television and the internet was beginning to challenge print media. Satellite radio was also growing in popularity, but had not become a rival to fm radio. By the turn of the century, print media, network television, cable television and satellite radio were all being challenged by the all-encompassing internet.

Access to multi-media through electronic gadgets and devices has become a "perceived" necessity for most Americans and citizens of western civilization. The ever-changing cost of access to multi-media along with its gadgets and devices are not affordable expenses within the American family's median income budget in relation to other household priorities. However, virtually every American has managed to find a way to partake in this societal standard.

SUBTLE SUGGESTIONS

The media industry has mastered the art of suggestion through sending messages that are designed to be received by our sub consciousness, often undetected by our consciousness. Common messages conveyed by advertisers include:

1. Here is a problem that affects you
2. This is how you want to feel
3. This will make you feel better
4. You are being held back
5. You deserve better
6. Just do what feels right
7. Just follow instructions and obey

The general public is constantly bombarded with these messages from every direction. This is designed to reinforce uniformed responses from consumers that are exposed to these messages. The power of suggestion has been the most devastating weapon used against mankind since the Garden of Eden. In light of its current impact through media, it seems that this weapon has proven to be just as effective as it has ever been. The power of suggestion guides the consciousness of the mainstream world and utterly controls the simple minded. The scriptures say that the simple minded see danger but keep going and face the consequences as a result.

[Proverbs 26:12]

TRANSPORTATION

Personal transportation has been used to define one's status since the beginning of mankind. The first form of transportation involved taming animals like camels, elephants and horses to be ridden. After the invention of the wheel, animal drawn carriages like chariots and wagons became the standard of transportation sought after on land. Vessels used to travel by sea, and ultimately by air, have always been considered as extraordinary and/or privileged forms of transportation.

In the early part of the 20th century, the "affordable" automobile was introduced to the American public by Henry Ford. Ford pioneered the concept of mass production by assembly line with the black Model-T. When asked if he would provide a variety of colors he responded by saying that "You could get a Model-T in any color you wanted, as long as it is black". Ford's philosophy was to make modern transportation affordable and available to average American Families. Mass production of identical parts for one model was Ford's formula for low-cost manufacturing.

In contrast, the founders of General Motors (GM) promoted choice and discontentment by making a number of different models to choose from and changing features each year as to portray older models as undesirable by default because of the availability of a "new and improved" model. GM forced the automobile industry to follow suit with the exploitation of the American public's "inalienable right" to pursue happiness. Cars became social status symbols rather than need and value driven purchases. The bankruptcy of GM in 2009 and the continued "uninterrupted" operation of the Ford Motor Company seems to indicate that GM was fully committed to a philosophy that ultimately failed while Ford somehow managed to hold on to some of its founding principles, making it possible for them to survive.

LIFESTYLE

The U.S. has become the world leader when it comes to trend setting. Our economy has become dependent on convincing the rest of the world that our ways are the standards to be sought after in order to be recognized and accepted as "successful". Control of the media is control of the people. We are constantly being fed images that suggest to us: what to eat, what to wear, what consumer goods to buy, what to watch on television, what music to listen to, what books to read, what kind of car to drive, what kind of home to buy, and the list goes on.

From adolescence into adulthood, our society (primarily through media) promotes concepts like:

- Sex is okay as long as you practice "safe sex".

- It's okay to drink and get drunk as long as you drink responsibly and don't drive drunk.
- If you have an unwanted pregnancy, it's okay to have an abortion as a form of birth control (without having to consult with anyone).
- Access to credit is a form of personal wealth.
- Image is everything, fake it until you make it.

We are conditioned to feel deprived if we do not partake in the latest trends as suggested by the media. God's truth has been pre-empted by popular culture in today's U.S. society.

[2 Timothy 3:1-7]

CHAPTER IV

THE CARTER YEARS 1976 – 1980 [D]

HUMAN RIGHTS CHAMPION WITH AN AGENDA

FROM FARMING TO PRESIDENT

James Earl Carter, Jr. (born October 1, 1924) is an American politician and member of the Democratic Party who served as the 39th President of the United States from 1977 to 1981 and was awarded the 2002 Nobel Peace Prize, the only U.S. President to have received the Prize after leaving office. Before he became President, Carter served as a U.S. Naval officer, was a peanut farmer, served two terms as a Georgia State Senator and one as the Governor of Georgia, from 1971 to 1975.

ACCELERATED DESTRUCTION OF AMERICAN AGRICULTURE AND WATER SUPPLY

GENETICALLY ENGINEERED FOOD

During the Carter administration, there was significant emphasis placed on addressing world hunger through enhanced growing methods in agriculture. There were major advancements in the area of genetically engineering seed with the Monsanto Corporation leading the way.

Genetically Modified Organisms (known as GMO's) are alterations to natural (organic) properties at an atomic level to produce a new strain of the organism. Adding pesticides to seed was one of the most pervasive and intrusive and controversial actions taken with GMO's in the agricultural sector. The stated intensions were to produce a higher-yield of crop resulting from reduced losses by insects and rodents. The risk was that the amount of organic crops produced would be dramatically reduced due to higher cost in comparison to cheap GMO foods and cross-pollination from GMO growers to Organic farms.

FOOD STOCKPILING AND GLOBAL HUMANITARIANISM

There was a great deal of food surplus in America during this administration. The U.S. government stockpiled food (mainly grain and seed) in various warehouses, silos, and even caves. Consequently, our government used these surpluses to export food to needy countries around the world. With the advent of GMO's, we grew crops exponentially to replenish our normal food supply needs with enough left over to export and stockpile.

WATER DEPLETION

The vast majority of our food supply is produced in the Midwest commonly referred to as "America's Bread Basket". This area primarily includes the states of Illinois, Indiana, Iowa, Kansas, Michigan, Minnesota, Missouri, Ohio, Nebraska, North Dakota, South Dakota and Wisconsin.

The Ogallala Aquifer is the nation's largest water table aquifer which is located in the Midwest directly under portions of these main agricultural areas in the region. It is a well-known fact that this aquifer is being depleted from decades of intense irrigation for agricultural activities. This matter is further complicated by the fact that ground water converted into crops is being exported to other countries resulting in total water displacement from the continental U.S.

Another impact to this aquifer comes from oil and coal extraction process commonly known as "fracking". In this process, water is used as a hydraulic injection fluid into the earth creating fractures resulting in the release of oil and natural gas. There are two primary long-term impacts resulting from this process. Vast amounts of groundwater is being used which affects our drinking water supply and disposal of injection water contaminates drinking water sources during disposal.

EXPANSION OF THE SOCIAL JUSTICE AGENDA

HUMAN RIGHTS

Habitat for Humanity

Habitat for Humanity International is a Non-Governmental Organization (NGO) founded in 1976 in Americus, Georgia. Their stated main mission is to promote and facilitate housing that is "simple, decent and affordable" in lower income communities around the world. This process is designed to be executed primarily by volunteers. Habitat has become the largest non-profit builder in the world. President Carter has promoted Habitat from its inception and has participated in building projects around the world spanning over the decades since leaving office.

His continued commitment to matters relating to promoting peaceful solutions to conflicts, Human Rights and Social Justice worldwide after leaving the office of U.S. President earned him a Noble Peace Prize in 2002.

NATURAL OR MAN-MADE DISASTERS / PHENOMENA: 1976 - 1980

There were significant natural disasters and/or notable phenomena that took place during this period of time, including, but not limited to:

- The Three Mile Island nuclear accident
- The 1980 eruption of Mount St. Helens in Washington state

TECHNOLOGICAL EVENTS: 1976 - 1980

There were a number of events and milestones in technology that took place during this period of time, including, but not limited to:

- Apple, Inc. was founded in 1976 (side-note: Microsoft was founded in 1975).
- Bell Labs produced the Single-Chip Digital Signal Processor (DSP) in 1979.

POLITICAL EVENTS: 1976 - 1980

Notable events in U.S. politics that took place throughout the late 1970's include:

- The Iranian Revolution took place in 1979. Iran becomes an Islamic republic under the Grand Ayatollah Ruhollah Khomeini replacing the Shaw of Iran as the country's leader.
- The 1979–1981 Iran hostage crisis
- The 1979 energy crisis
- In 1979 President Carter merged several disaster response agencies into one Federal Emergency Management Agency (FEMA) by executive order.
- The United States boycott of the 1980 Summer Olympics in Moscow (which was the only U.S. boycott in Olympic history)
- In 1979 President Carter was the first American president to authorize covert support for the Mujahadeen in Afghanistan to fight against Soviet threats. This group would eventually birth a new organization known as the Taliban. This organization has been cited as a terrorist group opposed to U.S. foreign policy and an affiliate with other mainline Islamic Extremist terrorist groups like Al-Qaida who was blamed for the 911 attacks.
- The Soviet invasion of Afghanistan
- Control of the U.S. built Panama Canal was returned to Panama.
- Establishment of the Camp David Accords which is a long-term peace agreement between Egypt and Israel.
- Establishment of two-new cabinet-level departments being; Department of Energy and the Department of Education.
- There were broad expansions to the Animal Welfare Act as Amendments in 1976.

CHAPTER V

The Reagan Years 1980 – 1988 [R]

THE U.S. BECOMES THE LAST SUPERPOWER

CHANGING THE PARADIGM OF MODERN POLITICS

In 1980 Ronald Reagan won the Republican nomination for President. With former Texas Congressman and U.N. Ambassador George H.W. Bush as his running mate, he defeated the incumbent Democratic president, Jimmy Carter in the general election by a "landslide". Ronald Reagan's presidency was characterized by "peace through strength" from the very beginning when his inauguration into office triggered the release of the American hostages in Iran who had been held for several months during the previous Carter administration. This was considered as the first of many responses from world leaders around the globe to the message that President Reagan had been sending throughout his presidential campaign regarding his willingness to use U.S. military might for promoting capitalism and democracy around the world in the name of peace, prosperity and freedom.

America was poised for dominance around the world by becoming the last superpower. The Reagan administration encouraged innovation and entrepreneurship in America by obtaining an overhaul of the U.S. tax code from congress, which eliminated many deductions and exempted millions of people with low incomes. Capital gains taxes were reduced and strategic areas of the banking sector were deregulated to a great extent, allowing undercapitalized banking institutions of all kinds to partake in risky transaction in the name of prosperity and growth of the U.S. marketplace.

U.S. MILITARY BUILD-UP

The Reagan administration was fully committed to building up America's armed forces. The defense budget was increased by over 1/3 which was unprecedented during peace time. As a result of the increase in defense spending, America's armed forces were unmatched by any other military in the world.

The Soviet Union was considered to be the only formidable match to the U.S. as a world superpower because of the size of its army and its nuclear weapon arsenal. President Reagan announced the "Star Wars" missile defense program in conjunction with the space shuttle program. These leaps of technology catapulted the "perceived" invincibility of the American military. President Reagan's investment into the American space program, NASA, caused a shift in the balance of world power.

The Soviet Union was in no position to compete with the U.S. technologically nor economically. As a result, President Reagan and Soviet Prime Minister Mikhail Gorbachev negotiated a treaty that would eliminate intermediate-range nuclear missiles. This ultimately led to the end of the Cold War, the fall of the Berlin wall and the break-up of the Soviet Union.

REAGANOMICS

"Reaganomics" was a term coined by Paul Harvey, who was a popular media figure at the time of the Reagan presidency. The term refers to the "unique" economic policies promoted and implemented by President Reagan.

The primary objectives of Reaganomics were:

1. Reduction of taxes on income and capital gains
2. Reduction of government regulation to increase free market
3. Control inflation through control of capital availability

Other common terms associated with these policies were "Trickle-down economics" and "Supply-side economics."

Trickle-down economics depicts the effect of providing the wealthiest members of society and business with tax cuts and incentives which would lead to an expanding economy that would ultimately produce a financial trickle-down effect to the poorest members of society in various ways. Supply-side economics depicts the effect of boosting production as a means of encouraging consumer spending which would lead to economic stimulation and growth.

Many economists believe that these policies favored the wealthy and left it up to a relatively select few to decide the fate of everyone else. The biggest problem with Trickle-down economics is that human nature makes those who have wealth desire to have more, even in a bad economy. In recent history, the wealthy have found many ways to protect their wealth from downturns through "loophole extractions" such as in the case of sureties being bailed out by the federal government. Once secured, wealthy people will not typically re-invest without incentives and relative guarantees. Thus, banks are not likely to make loans that are not "heavily" collateralized by hard-assets with "recognizable" value and personal cash for added protection as they must work in the best interest of their largest depositors.

THE MILLENNIAL GENERATION: HIP-HOP CULTURE

Hip-Hop or "Rap" took the music industry and civil society by storm in the early 1980's. At first, this African American born style of music was only popular in urban minority communities. However, a group called The Sugar Hill Gang released a song called "Rapper's Delight" that became the first rap song to cross-over into the pop category and reach #1 on the billboards. Many would follow, giving way to the emergence of the Hip-Hop culture.

Hip-Hop started as an art form that reflected real life in the inner-cities of America. Rap music told the story of two-Americas. The U.S. government was telling a story of unprecedented peace and prosperity that included the American dream of homeownership, social, technological, and industrial advancements, increased wages and boundless opportunities for all. Hip-Hop was telling a different story of suffering and despair, rampant drug use, poverty and violence in the urban communities of America's largest cities like New York, Los

Angeles, Houston, Philadelphia and Detroit to name a few. The Hip-Hop message resonated with suburban youth that felt disconnected from their parents that were consumed with pursuing the American dream to realize that their children were being raised by an agenda-driven media, which was being taken over by Hip-Hop and music videos, started by MTV.

Hip-Hop turned into the culture of a generation known as "Y" or the Millennials. Millions of young people around the country that did not live in urban Hip-Hop communities began to emulate the lifestyle. This movement eventually became pervasive, crossing ethnic, cultural and generational boundaries, ultimately expanding to the international arena. Hip-Hop became so popular that many Christian organizations adopted Hip-Hop approaches to their youth outreach ministries in order to relate to their own youth.

THE GHETTO LIFE PHENOMENA

The downside to this movement is that its origins come from "Ghetto Life" which involved various forms of rampant violence drug use, poverty, moral degradation, fatherless families and despair. Many characters from these communities became glorified for their wrongdoings and relentless pursuit of fame and fortune at any cost. One of the culture's most renowned celebrities made popular the phrase "get rich or die trying."

This movement emerged at a time when Black and Latino males were being incarcerated in over 3:1 ratios compared to white males. This was a staggering statistic considering that Blacks and Latinos combined still represented the minority with regards to population but yet represented the vast majority of inmates in the U.S. prison system. In big cities throughout the U.S. like, New York, Los Angeles, Chicago, Philadelphia and Washington D.C., over half the population of Black and Latino males between the ages of 12 and 24 had an arrest record. Most were from lower income communities in or near public housing complexes that were often referred to as ghettos.

Consequently, the endorsement and wholesale promotion of the prison lifestyle became the hallmark image for the Hip Hop culture. Prison life was projected to Hip Hop audience which ironically was mostly made up of youth and young adults between the ages of 12 and 24. In essence, the U.S. produced a generation that glorified wrongdoing and the concept of "easy money" through becoming a criminal, professional athlete or entertainer. This phenomenon eventually found its way around world, making inroads with the youth of various cultures. The fast-moving social impact of Hip Hop on youth around the world was unlike any that had been seen since the Hippie movement of the previous generation. However, its rapid pervasiveness was "unprecedented" due to the internet and social media technology providing access to billions worldwide. America was seen by many nations and governments as an exporter of Hip Hop culture, which was like a rapidly spreading virus because of its ability to infect the minds of a society's youth, challenge and corrupt moral standards and its potential for civil disruption.

About this same time, literacy rates among school students in America had reached record lows and High school drop-out rates soared in conjunction with prayer being taken out of the public school system and the concept of creation being replaced by evolution. The U.S. education system was not "effectively" reaching this generation as in the past. The gap between literate and illiterate widened as technology grew and computers were added to the equation.

CRACK COCAINE IN AMERICA

During the Hip Hop revolution, Crack cocaine had been introduced to the urban streets of our nation's major cities in the early 1980's. Crack was a cheap cocaine by-product that was made in makeshift laboratories called "Crack-Houses" by members of local drug cartels. At the time, Crack was considered to be the least expensive, most addictive and deadliest narcotic ever distributed in America. Crack attics became commonly characterized as capable of doing anything to get enough money to fund their next high. However, other than illegal drug possession and use, Crack attics engaged in petty theft more than any other type of crime by far. was There were numerous accounts of Crack attics as being like "Zombies" that were "possessed" by the drug which drove them to steal "anything" from "anyone" at "anytime" in an attempt to acquire enough money to buy more Crack. Ironically, Crack attics were also known to attempt selling "anything" to "anyone" at "anytime" with reckless regard for being accused of theft or being caught by police.

Getting Crack off the streets was not a major priority to government and law enforcement while Crack was considered as an inner-city minority community problem. As the urban experience was invited to suburban America, initially for the music, secondly the culture, it gave way to the increase of access to inner-city drugs, like crack cocaine, to suburban youth. Crack cocaine gave way to the rise and popularity of other cheap synthetic drugs like "crank" and "Crystal Meth" that subsequently became popular in suburban communities.

THE EMERGENCE OF THE TALIBAN AND AL-QAEDA

In the late 1970's, Afghan opposition groups rebelled against the Soviet-backed Afghan government known as the Democratic Republic of Afghanistan (DRA), which was in power at the time. The U.S. started to provide support to the rebels under the Carter administration. This support was continued and "significantly" increased during the Reagan administration. U.S. support for the Afghan rebels against the spread of communism by the Soviets ultimately led to the "Reagan Doctrine". The U.S. supplied the rebels with military arms. It is "alleged" that the rebels received training from the C.I.A. These rebels later went on to become known as the

Taliban. Another group by the name of Al-Qaeda emerged as a trained fighting force resulting from this conflict as well.

TECHNOLOGICAL EVENTS: 1980 - 1988

There were a number of milestones in technology that took place during this period of time, including, but not limited to:

- NASA launches the Space Shuttle program in 1981
- TCP/IP (Transmission Control Protocol and Internet Protocol) is established
- Cisco Systems was founded in 1984
- Microsoft and IBM join forces
- Apple introduces Macintosh
- Microsoft introduces Windows 1.0
- America Online (AOL) is born

POLITICAL EVENTS: 1980 - 1988

Among the notable events in U.S. politics that took place throughout the 1980's, they include:

- Weapons were being sold to Iran to help facilitate the release of U.S. hostages being held by Hezbollah in Lebanon. Proceeds from the arms sales would be used to support of the Contra rebels (through the CIA) in their mission to overthrow the Nicaraguan government that was controlled by the socialist Sandinista regime. President Reagan was found to be "direct-knowledge" of this operation with Iran, who was the subject of an arms embargo by the U.S. at the time. This became known as the "Iran-Contra Affair".

CHAPTER VI

THE BUSH #41 YEARS 1988 – 1992 [R]

EXPANSION OF FOREIGN POLICY AND FREE TRADE

HEIR TO THE REAGAN DYNASTY

In 1988 Bush won the Republican nomination for President and, with Senator Dan Quayle of Indiana as his running mate. He defeated Massachusetts Governor Michael Dukakis in the general election. Bush's election into office was viewed by many as an attempt by the American people to extend the prosperity, peace and strength established by his predecessor. However, Bush was faced with the unavoidable reality of the country's growing budget deficit which was, primarily due to the Regan administration's increased military spending and tax cuts. America's major cities were experiencing high crime rates and budget restraints, which are common fallout results of major growth and economic development.

Many believed that Bush, having strong ties to the Texas oil industry, gave special priority to matters that related to the petroleum industry during his administration. Bush made significant progress in foreign policy by making efforts to forge good relations between the U.S. and China, to whom he had been an ambassador prior to taking office with the Reagan administration.

Bush was also known for initiating important domestic policies such as the war on drugs. Tougher laws were established against drug dealers and anyone in possession of drugs with emphasis on crack cocaine. He promoted increases in federal spending for local law enforcement agencies and launched a series of military operations against Central and South American drug lords. Most notable, U.S. troops were sent to Nicaragua to overthrow the government and capture its leader, Manuel Noriega. The corruption of the Panamanian Government and its support of the drug Cartels under President Noriega were well known throughout the world. Noriega was captured and brought back to the U.S. and tried in federal court as a drug trafficker.

The first Lady, Barbara Bush became popular for her interest and efforts toward improving the nation's grade school educational system. The No Child Left Behind (NCLB) act was proposed by President Bush (41). This Bill later became law under Bush (43).

THE GULF WAR

In the early 1990's, the Iraqi military invaded Kuwait, then threatened to move into Saudi Arabia under the ruling authority of Iraqi President Saddam Hussein. Bush immediately responded to the threat by launching operation "Dessert Storm", which sent almost a half-million U.S. Troops to liberate Kuwait and ward off any threats against the Kingdom of Saudi Arabia. Within less than a week, the Iraqi forces were driven out of Kuwait. Bush was heavily criticized for not sending troops into the Iraqi capital city of Bagdad to capture Saddam Husain. Because of the dictator's reputation for threatening his neighboring countries sovereignty and brutal atrocities against his own people, most believed that the U.S. would eventually have to return to Iraq to finish the job.

NAFTA

NAFTA is an acronym for the North Atlantic Free Trade Agreement. This agreement originated in the late 1980's with a similar agreement between the U.S. and Canada. President Bush approached the Mexican government about the creation of a free trade agreement between the U.S. and Mexico. Canada expressed interest in being included and was added to the process. Late in his term as president, Bush was able to successfully complete the negotiations for NAFTA while the next American president would ratify the agreement and put it into practice.

U.S. RELATIONSHIP WITH ISRAEL CHALLENGED BY MUSLIM CRUDE

Middle Eastern affairs have always been of interest to the U.S. as a Christian nation. Since the land of Israel was given back to the Jews from British control in the 1940's, protecting Israel's right to exist as a nation among its Arab neighbors and supporting the Israeli Defense Force (IDF) with the latest and most advanced American weapons was our primary focus in the region. As a result, Israel eventually gained access to nuclear weapons. Israel has used its nuclear status to ward off any notion of a unified Islamic Invasion against their sovereign state.

In order to meet the growing energy needs of the ever-expanding American economy, assuring access to crude supplies in the Middle East became a "heightened" priority for the Bush administration. The U.S. petroleum industry was losing its leverage to the Organization of the Petroleum Exporting Countries (a.k.a. OPEC) which was a consortium of state sponsored petroleum companies. However, the military strength of most OPEC countries was tied to a superpower like the U.S., China or the former Soviet Union. President Bush, along with U.S. oil companies, strengthened ties with the Kingdom of Saudi Arabia (KSA) government. With U.S. refinery technology and innovation, the KSA would continue to lead OPEC as the world's top producer of crude oil.

NOTE: OPEC is an acronym for the Organization of the Petroleum Exporting Countries. The organization is currently made up of twelve members: Algeria, Angola, Ecuador, Iran, Iraq, Kuwait, Libya, Nigeria, Qatar, Saudi Arabia, the United Arab Emirates and Venezuela.

This group originated with the government of Venezuela approaching the Middle-Eastern oil producing countries governments about forming a cartel consisting of major oil producers from around the world that were disadvantaged in negotiating on crude export prices to the major oil companies that controlled the petroleum industry.

As a gesture of good will, the U.S. supplies the KSA with security from the U.S. military and U.S. made weapons, primarily to defend U.S. interest against the threat of invasion from Iraq and its tyrannical ruler Saddam Husain along with the ever-looming threat posed by Iran being led by radical Islamic clerics. The U.S. government and U.S. oil companies also strengthened relationships with other OPEC members throughout the region including; the United Arab Emirates (UAE), Kuwait and Qatar. Iraq was viewed as a politically "unstable" member of OPEC in the region known to possess large "untapped" deposits of crude, potentially equal to or greater than that of the KSA. Serving the interest of both Israel and the oil-rich Arab nations has become increasingly difficult for the U.S. government as Muslim sentiments remain hostile toward the Jews.

[Luke16:13 NIV]

GLOBAL DISCONTENT WITH U.S. POPULAR CULTURE

America had flourished economically and militarily under the Reagan administration. The American president was considered as the most powerful person on the planet and the leader of the free world. Through exponential leaps in technology and satellite communications, the U.S. promoted the spread of democracy and capitalism along with its brand of popular culture around the globe like no other society in the history of the world.

Many nations around the world, mostly third-world governments and developing nations, viewed capitalism as abhorrent because of the great disparities created between extreme wealth and extreme poverty in free-market economic systems. Many others, mostly Islamic states, believed that capitalism was a catalyst for moral degradation, referring to Americans as "Infidels". As the American economy grew, so did contempt for the "decadent" and often "immoral" American lifestyle that was being portrayed as the highest standard of living in the world. There was growing dissension within the KSA between the religious leaders and the country's Royal Family about its close-knit relationship with the U.S. government. The Kingdom of Saudi Arabia and its Royal Family are considered to be the keepers of the faith for the Islamic religion, recognized by all Muslims worldwide. The irony is that the U.S. was being despised by Muslims for its rampant immorality rather than its claim to Christianity.

RAPID GROWTH FOR ISLAM AND CHRISTIANITY

As a result of the perceived posture of "arrogance" among displayed by Americans, Islam was becoming one of the fastest growing religions around the world, largely by default. Christianity in America had become "significantly" marginalized, especially in Muslim nations, by the rapid increase of powerful "mega-Churches" in the U.S. that were widely viewed as biased toward capitalism through their messages of financial prosperity being portrayed as "alignment" with "Godlincss". This period is known as the "Prosperity Movement" in American Church history. Many citizens of non-Christian or non-religious secular countries, like Rwanda and Somalia, which were forsaken or neglected by the U.S. government, became disenfranchised with the prosperity movement in the American Christian Church.

Even more devastating was the wave of mainstream Christian leaders falling from their positions as a result of immoral behavior which was viewed by many as evidence of the American Church being filled with hypocrisy. Islam portrayed itself as a "moral" and "consistent" religion for all people. Islam grew in spite of being known to subjugate unwilling converts by force and respond with extreme consequences against any who resisted, often resulting in violent acts of terrorism and atrocities against ethnic or religious groups. The "inclusive" and "moral" message of Islam was being seen more as a viable alternative to many who were disenfranchised with the American brand of Capitalistic Christianity that emerged from the prosperity movement. This also gave way to significant growth in other religions.

However, other brands of Christianity took a more conservative, inclusive and compassionate approach to ministry, which grew "exponentially" around the world. The American Church was financially stable and made "enormous" investments into foreign ministries and missions from virtually "ALL BRANDS" of Christianity. Though flawed, the American Church, as a whole, was recognized around the world for its generosity. Consequently, the gospel was spread around the world and Christianity grew exponentially as the number of Christians in America started to decline.

TECHNOLOGICAL EVENTS: 1988 - 1992

There were a number of milestones in technology that took place during this period of time, including, but not limited to:

- The World Wide Web is born
- AOL adds "Chat Rooms" to its service
- Internet browsers Netscape Navigator and Internet Explorer were born
- Web Crawler was born (The first full-text internet search engine) followed by Yahoo and Google
- Cell phones with internet access were introduced by Nokia
- Apple introduces the I-Pod

POLITICAL EVENTS: 1988-1992

Among the notable events in U.S. politics that took place throughout the late 1980's and early 1990's, they include:

- Chief Justice Clarence Thomas was appointed to the U.S. Supreme Court by President Bush after a drawn out confirmation hearing by the U.S. Senate surrounding allegations of sexual harassment were made against Thomas by his former aide Anita Hill.

- President Bush spoke out against violent Rap music lyrics promoting the killing of police officers

CHAPTER VII

THE CLINTON YEARS 1992 – 2000 [D]

DOMESTIC POLICY REFORM AND URBAN REVITALIZATION

PRESIDENT OF THE PEOPLE

Former governor of Arkansas, William (Bill) Jefferson Clinton along with his running mate, former congressman from Tennessee, Al Gore, Jr. defeated the incumbent George H.W. Bush to become the 42nd U.S. president. President Clinton was well spoken and well received by the majority of Americans, even winning the support of independents and some republicans. He had an uncanny ability to "connect" with average people while maintaining a strong intellectual posture at the highest levels of interaction with heads of state from around the world. He was particularly popular within the African-American community dubbed as "the first black president." Bill Clinton was a true president of the people.

President Clinton realized that he was elected to devote his primary attention on the American people rather than foreign policy. Some may say that the Clinton administration did as much for the American people at a community level to support sustainable communities as the Reagan administration did to grow the U.S. economy.

WELFARE REFORM

The Clinton administration brought an end to the concept of perpetual welfare being passed down from generation to generation as an institutional way of life. Many job training programs along with welfare to work initiatives were created. These programs targeted at-risk youth, under educated adults and recipients of public assistance.

A program called Hope VI was created to help revitalize communities by demolishing outdated public housing complexes and rebuilding the community with reduced density. The rebuilt community would have a mix of low-income and market rate rental units along with affordable home units for sale. This was designed to reverse the effects from decades of densely-populated and impoverished communities that had adversely affected the surrounding neighborhoods and their home values.

COMMUNITY REDEVELOPMENT

The Enterprise Community (EC) program was created to establish a system geared toward urban revitalization. Qualified communities in every urban setting around the country were designated as ECs by the federal government through the department of Housing and Urban Development (HUD). Each designated EC would form a Community Redevelopment Agency (CRA) that would act as a liaison between HUD and community based Public-Private Partnerships (P3s). The CRA and select P3s would devise ways of revitalizing its urban communities. The P3s would apply for and receive federal subsidies for these projects as funds became available throughout the year from HUD.

AFFORDABLE HOUSING

Local banks partnered with these P3s by providing lines of credit and construction loans along with home loans being made available to qualified buyers. What made this program unique from conventional real estate development was that the P3s were building in communities that would not support new home construction due to the appraisal requirements for conventional financing. HUD would provide the P3 with a pool of funds that could be used for land acquisition and offered to home buyers as a Deferred Payment Loan (DPL).

In essence, the homebuyer would purchase a new home for a price "well-over" its appraised value. The difference between what the banks would lend and the selling price would be bridged by a DPL from HUD. The homebuyers would be told that due to the overall revitalization plan taking place throughout a particular community that values would eventually rise and catch up with the purchase price. The selling point was that in most cases, the DPL was forgiven in 15 years. It looked like free money to the homebuyer. Minority communities were targeted because "statistically" they were not as likely to move or upgrade during the term of the DPL.

These programs were likely contributing factors in the sudden rise of home prices and perceived increase of values at this particular time. Most Hope VI and EC redevelopment projects were located in densely populated urban areas in or near major cities. Many of these projects were in or adjacent to downtown business districts and high-rent areas. Developers perceived that neighboring properties had increased in value as a result of the blight being removed from these areas which contributed to the increase in home prices. There were a number of investors, particularly "day traders", rapidly gaining great wealth as a result of the dot com bubble. Many decided to diversify their investment portfolios with U.S. real estate. This wealth infusion contributed to a growing U.S. housing market.

The tactics used by P3s participating in the HUD affordable housing program establishing "artificial" home price inflation would eventually become merged into the mainstream housing marketplace due to a perfect storm of events and conditions. The "resetting" of affordable home prices through urban redevelopment projects would play a significant role in creating the housing value bubble in the early stages of the U.S. housing crisis.

COMMUNITY POLICING

The Clinton administration promoted the concept of community policing as a part of the overall community redevelopment initiative. This program involved adding new police officers given the specific task of carrying out the Community Oriented Policing (COP) program. The COP program encouraged law enforcement officers to develop relationships with community residents and be available to neighborhood associations at all times. The idea was that the best way to combat urban crime was to get the law abiding citizens involved. This program was well-received and became very popular.

TECHNOLOGICAL EVENTS: 1992 - 2000

There were a number of milestones in technology that took place during this period of time, including, but not limited to:

- The digital answering machine was created
- The Pentium processor was invented
- The World Wide Web (www) internet protocol (HTTP) and the www language HTML was created
- The computer language Java was created
- Web TV became available to the public
- Google was established in 1998
- The drug Viagra was created
- American Pathfinder launched on its 310 million mile mission to Mars

POLITICAL EVENTS: 1992-2000

Among the notable events in U.S. politics that took place throughout the 1990's, they include:

- The Bill Clinton sex scandal with intern Monica Lewinski
- The impeachment of President Clinton

CHAPTER VIII

THE BUSH #43 YEARS 2000 – 2008 [R]

FAITH, WAR AND ECONOMIC DEVASTATION

THE PROMISE OF BIPARTISAN LEADERSHIP

Former Texas Governor George W. Bush (son of former president George H.W. Bush) "narrowly" defeated former vice-president Al Gore in one of the most contested elections in U.S. history. The election was held on November 7th, 1999. It turned out that Gore had won the popular vote by less than 1%, Bush won by 5 electoral votes that were ultimately obtained by a controversial victory in Florida. The Florida votes were so close that the Gore campaign called for a recount. A recount was done and Bush was reported to have retained his lead by only 327 votes. There would be accusations, petitions, motions, actions and lawsuits filed for approximately four weeks after the election with regards to vote counting in Florida, which was a republican state whose governor was Jeb Bush, the republican candidate's brother. On December 13th, 1999, thirty-six days after the election, Gore finally conceded to Bush and publicly acknowledged his defeat. On January 20th, 2000, George W. Bush would become the 43rd president of the United States of America along with his vice-president Dick Cheney. Bush and Cheney were re-elected in 2004 to serve a second term, defeating his opponent Massachusetts Senator John Kerry and his running partner John Edwards.

Bush had come to Washington with a reputation for bipartisanship in his governance over the state of Texas. The American public was hopeful that he would be capable of breaking partisan grid-lock that had taken hold in congress. He selected Ret. General Colin Powell to become the first African-American U.S. Secretary of State. President Bush immediately focused on bipartisan initiatives like the No Child Left Behind (NCLB) Act and the Medicare prescription drug benefit reform Act.

Much of G.W. Bush's political successes were attributed to his chief political advisor, Karl Rove, who had orchestrated his campaigns from his entry into politics. Rove is heralded as a "master political strategist" and "the Architect" of the Bush presidency.

THE CHRISTIAN EVANGELICAL PRESIDENT

President Bush was known to be a self-proclaimed born-again Evangelical Christian. His philosophical views were considered as conservative, promoting limited government, personal responsibility, strong families, along with the idea that government should be controlled at local levels. He reached out to the Christian community and gave unprecedented Whitehouse access to Christian Evangelical leaders. He created a new Faith-Based and Community Initiative which he dubbed as empowering America's Armies of Compassion.

President Bush promoted a culture of life and supported the pro-life movement. He appointed conservative pro-life judges, Chief Justice John Roberts and Justice Samuel Alito, to the U.S. Supreme Court. He initiated a global HIV/AIDS prevention and treatment campaign that was reported to have saved millions of lives in Africa and around the world. He renewed America's commitment to support and defend Israel's right to exist and considered her as an important ally to the U.S. in the Middle-East.

INHERITANCE OF A DECLINING ECONOMY

President Bush started his presidency with an economy heading toward recession. After the dot com bubble burst in 2000 the value of the U.S. dollar fell significantly. Foreign investors found themselves with additional wealth as the euro was "substantially" outperforming the dollar. Many foreign investors viewed their currency exchange dividends as an opportunity to invest in U.S. real estate. Home mortgages were being bundled into securities and offered to investors by Wall Street banks.

The results from years of unprecedented low income and capital gains taxes along with a growing federal budget deficit were beginning to take effect. He decided to initiate a tax cut for all taxpayers which was reportedly helped fuel job creation for 52 months. He expanded free trade by signing agreements with more than a dozen nations.

BIN-LADEN DECLARES WAR AGAINST THE U.S.

SEPTEMBER 11TH, 2001

On September 11th, 2001, an Islamic extremist group called Al-Qaeda, led by Osama Bin-Laden, declared a "holy-war" (a.k.a. Jihad) against the United States of America. Bin-Laden orchestrated a coordinated attack against the United States through highly-trained terrorist cells successfully hijacking three commercial airliners simultaneously. The planes were used as missiles targeting the World trade Center in New York, the White House and the Pentagon in Washington, D.C.

The attacks were successful, killing over 3,000 American citizens along with many foreigners. Bin-Laden's attack was the first against the U.S. by a foreign enemy that took place on mainland American soil in our nation's history. Al-Qaeda had successfully exploited vulnerability within the most powerful nation on the planet.

Bin-Laden's stated goal was to strike terror in the hearts of Americans through random acts of violence and destruction geared toward destabilization of the American economy. He believed that the average American citizen had become weak and feeble over time as a result of our nation becoming a consumer-based society since World War II. The war in Viet-Nam and the U.S. withdrawal without victory had set precedence for the use of terrorism combined with guerilla warfare as an effective means of battling the U.S. The concept of using suicide bombers or "Jihadists" to lead the offensives against the enemy in battle was enhanced and expanded by Al-Qaeda because it makes distinguishing the enemy from the general public very difficult.

THE WAR ON TERRORISM

The concept of "War on Terrorism" was first used by President Ronald Reagan against the Sandinistas in the mid 1980's. The Sandinistas were a socialist party that led Nicaraguan resistance against U.S. occupation in the 1930's by use of guerrilla warfare tactics under General Augusto Cesar Sandino. President George W. Bush expanded the concept to a "Global" War on Terrorism directed against any organized group of people expressing the desire to commit acts of terror having demonstrated the ability to carry out such threats. This war was primarily focused on Al-Qaeda, led by Osama Bin-Laden, who was believed to be the master mind behind the September 11th attacks. This focus was extended to include the Taliban in Afghanistan, who was believed to be an affiliate organization that was aiding and harboring Bin-Laden. As a result of Bin-Laden's claim that his attack was considered to be a declaration of a holy war on the U.S., all Muslim extremist organizations were being considered as potential enemy combatants. Shortly after the September 11th attacks, Bush made controversial statements characterizing the war on terrorism as a "Crusade" and named countries that he considered as the "Axis of Evil". His statements were widely viewed as "religious" and "anti-Muslim" which substantiated Bin-Laden's claim of holy war among Muslim extremists.

HISTORY OF RELATIONSHIP BETWEEN THE U.S. AND IRAQ

Efforts toward U.S. – Iraqi relations extend as far back as the 1960's, with U.S. officials taking note of Saddam Hussein's rise to power as the leader of the Ba'ath Party and Iraqi government. Iraq and Iran had been engaged in border disputes for some time. Their dispute was solved in the mid 1970's. However, this gave way to the ongoing animosity of the Iraqi government toward the Kurds. As a result of the border dispute being resolved support to the Kurds through Iran was cut off, leading to atrocities being carried out against them. Saddam continued to use chemical weapons against the Kurds, which was a violation of international law, drawing condemnation from the U.S. and many other nations around the world.

Assistant Secretary of State for Near Eastern and South Asian Affairs Alfred L. Atherton, Jr. is on the record as saying "Hussein is a rather remarkable person ... he is running the show; and he's a very ruthless and ... pragmatic, intelligent power."

In the aftermath of the Iraq war, and the ongoing insurgence from rival factions throughout the country, it seems that another "Strongman Ruler" will likely rise to power again in order to "effectively" govern the nation of Iraq.

Despite the ongoing atrocities against the Kurds, in thc 1970's, Secretary of State Henry Kissinger engaged Iraqi Foreign Minister Hammadi regarding the potential of normalizing relations between the U.S. and Iraq as part of a broader campaign for strengthening relations between the U.S. and the Arab world as a whole. Hammadi expressed his sentiments against the U.S. support for the existence of Israel. Kissinger responds by stating that Israel's existence is not up for discussion. However, Kissinger is reported to have portrayed Israeli influence on U.S. policy as diminishing, due to changes in electoral laws. Hammadi and Kissinger discussed other regional issues and agreed there were no obstacles to improving bilateral relations.

Throughout the 1980's, the U.S. government and private companies established working relationships with the Iraqi government as a countermeasure to the Iranians and interest in Iraqi oil. However, Saddam Hussein proved to be too much of a political liability due to the continued atrocities committed by Iraq's use of chemical weapons against Iranians and the Kurds. By 1990, the U.S. had added Iraq to its list of state sponsors of terrorism. The UN became involved with this matter due to the violations against international law.

In the early 1990's, Iraq invaded the sovereign nation of Kuwait. Kuwait is a relatively small but oil rich nation on the southern border of Iraq. The U.S. responded to this act of aggression by sending approximately a half-million troops to liberate Kuwait under the name Operation Desert Storm. Iraqi forces were quickly driven from Kuwait by a multi-national coalition led by U.S. forces. This war between the U.S. coalition and Iraq was known as the Gulf war.

After the end of the Gulf war invasion of Kuwait, a portion of the U.S. led coalition remained in the region due to the continued threat from Iraq against its Arab neighbors. This operation was called Desert Shield. There were Iraqi no-fly zones imposed to protect the Kurdish minority and the Shi'a Arab population within Iraq. The Iraqi government was ordered to eliminate its chemical weapons capabilities and provide UN inspectors with unfettered access to facilities believed to be used in making or storing weapons of mass destruction (WMD).

Saddam remained defiant and continued to violate international laws and defy the international community. It was discovered that Saddam had initiated a plan to assassinate President George H.W. Bush. The plot was uncovered by U.S. intelligence and was averted. Throughout the 1990's, U.N. forces continued to apply sanctions and military pressure through special operations with the hope of getting the Iraqi government to comply with the rulings from the international community regarding WMD's in Iraq. In response to a U.S. military offensive in 1995 against Iraq named Operation Desert Fox, Iraq declared that it would not abide by the no-fly zones that had been imposed by the U.N. and shoot down Coalition aircraft. U.S. President Bill Clinton was convinced that Saddam Hussein was a menace to Iraq's neighboring countries and its own people due to his reported stockpile of WMD's and relentless attacks on the Kurds along with aggression against other Arab nations. Therefore, President George H.W. Bush signed the Iraq Liberation Act, in which he called for regime change in Iraq.

THE U.S. INVADES IRAQ

When President George W. Bush came into office in 2000, he increased the pressure being applied by the UN against Iraq by taking this matter to the United Nations Security Council (UNSC), seeking a resolution that would lead to forceful action being taken if the Iraqi government did not comply with previous demands regarding the WMD inspections.

The UNSC passed Resolution 1441, which offered Iraq a final opportunity to comply with its disarmament obligations or face serious consequences. However, UNSC resolution 1441 stopped short of authorizing the use of force by member states. In response to resolution 1441, the Iraqi government "unhurriedly" began to provide UN inspectors with access to alleged WMD storage sites throughout Iraq. The U.S. government continued to assert that the Iraqi government was being an obstruction as they "drug their feet" on this urgent matter.

After the September 11th attack on the U.S. by Al-Qaeda, the U.S. government was determined to respond with force against the enemy. Being that the enemy was a "mindset" rather than a nation, identifying a tangible and geographical representation for terrorism at its root was considered as an essential part of being able to defeat the opponent. Iraq was chosen by the Bush administration to be the initial target along with Afghanistan, where it was reported that Al-Qaeda leader Osama Bin-Laden had fled to.

In October 2002, the United States Congress authorized the president to use force, if necessary, to disarm Iraq. The congressional authorization was a bipartisan decision geared toward the U.S.

declaration of war on terrorism more than the enforcement of UNSC resolution 1441. There was stiff opposition from France, Russia, and China with regards to the use of force against Iraq, especially prior to the UN weapons inspectors having completed their inspections. Ultimately, the inspectors found no evidence of WMD production or storage. The U.S. claimed that Iraq was being deceptive by hiding the weapons in elaborate fortifications like underground bunkers under royal palaces.

The U.S. decided to initiate an invasion of Iraq to force regime change under the guides that such an action was lawful and in compliance with UNSC resolution 1441 which allowed for "serious consequences" as a result of non-compliance. Many have criticized President Bush for leading the U.S. to invade Iraq, citing that his decision was motivated by agendas other than the threat of Iraq expanding its production and use of chemical WMD's, such as:

- Control of Iraqi Oil
- Retaliation for assassination attempt against President George H.W. Bush
- Keeping Iraq from changing its reserve currency from dollars to Euros
- Stimulation of the American economy through war
- Testing of new U.S. military weapons and technology in combat
- Testing of U.S. mercenary armies known as "private contractors"

The Iraqi army was quickly defeated and the government was toppled in the process. On May 1, 2003, Bush announced that major combat operations in Iraq had ended. History would prove that this statement was premature. This tremendous error in judgment would haunt Bush throughout his remaining presidency. There was a protracted insurgency against the U.S. coalition forces, initially led by Ba'ath party loyalist and factions within the country seeking to establish power in the wake of the regime change initiative. Eventually, Al-Qaeda in Iraq would be formed and become a driving force behind much of the insurgency. Many more U.S. coalition soldiers died during the insurgency than during the initial invasion and battle phases leading up to the "premature" declaration by President Bush that major combat operations in Iraq had come to an end.

CREATION OF THE U.S. DEPARTMENT OF HOMELAND SECURITY

As a result of the September 11th attacks, the Department of Homeland Security (DHS) was created by President George W. Bush. Its primary responsibilities are to protect the U.S. homeland from terrorist attacks and responding to natural disasters.

The creation of DHS became the biggest government reorganization in American history. Many federal agencies were reorganized. DHS incorporates 22 government agencies into a single organization. Reorganization of the U.S. government to this extent has not taken place since the National Security Act (NSA) of 1947 which consolidated the War Department and Navy along with the newly created Air Force into a single Department of Defense under the Secretary of Defense. The NSA of 1947 also established the Central Intelligence Agency (CIA) and the National Security Council (NSC).

In March of 2002, the DHS initiated the Homeland Security Advisory System. A color-coded advisory alert scale would be publicized by a press release from the White House through the media. The intent was to advise the American public of any potential terror threats based on intelligence reports. However, it seen by the public as "unreliable" and was ultimately taken out of use.

THE USA PATRIOT ACT

The USA Patriot Act is described as an act to deter and punish terrorist acts in the United States and around the world, to enhance law enforcement investigatory tools, and other purposes. Congress has declared that this Act may be cited as **U**niting and **S**trengthening **A**merica by **P**roviding **A**ppropriate **T**ools **R**equired to **I**ntercept and **O**bstruct **T**errorism.

The Patriot Act is a "broad sweeping" piece of legislature that is designed to combat terrorism by any means necessary. The Act has ten original titles with numerous sections that describe scenarios that may be deemed as threats to the U.S. by the DHS and how its agents may do "virtually" whatever they deem as necessary to pursue an investigation of a person, group or entity that is suspected of connections to terrorist groups or activities.

USA PATRIOT ACT TITLES

I. ENHANCING DOMESTIC SECURITY AGAINST TERRORISM

II. ENHANCED SURVEILLANCE PROCEDURES

III. INTERNATIONAL MONEY LAUNDERING ABATEMENT AND ANTI-TERRORIST FINANCING ACT OF 2001

IV. PROTECTING THE BORDER

V. REMOVING OBSTACLES TO INVESTIGATING TERRORISM

VI. PROVIDING FOR VICTIMS OF TERRORISM, PUBLIC SAFETY OFFICERS, AND THEIR FAMILIES

VII. INCREASED INFORMATION SHARING FOR CRITICAL INFRASTRUCTURE PROTECTION

VIII. STRENGTHENING THE CRIMINAL LAWS AGAINST TERRORISM

IX. IMPROVED INTELLIGENCE

X. MISCELLANEOUS

There were concerns being expressed by many political groups and average American citizens regarding the unregulated power that was being given to the DHS through the Patriot Act. There have been allegations of Fourth Amendment constitutional violations regarding privacy rights in the form of wire-tapping and seizure of phone records without a warrant among other charges.

There are those in the Church who are concerned that the Patriot Act is constructed in such a way that it can be applied to any group of people that are deemed as an "ideological" threat to the U.S. and those who may be in support of such a group. This could technically be applied to so-called "Christian Extremists" in the same way that it targets "Muslim Extremists". If the rights of innocent Muslims in the U.S. are violated under the Patriot Act while a Christian president is in office, what prevents the rights of innocent Christians being violated under non-religious U.S. government leadership? Furthermore, Israel is always at risk of being deemed as a combatant state by a secular U.S. leader in a globalized society as their sovereignty relies heavily on Christian influence within the U.S. government.

THE MILLENNIAL WEALTH EXCHANGE PART-1: THE HOUSING BUBBLE

After September 11th, 2001, the American economy went into a tail spin. The government immediately responded with efforts to promote consumer spending and stimulate the market. The Federal Reserve (The Fed) responded with lowering the prime lending rates to banks. Wall Street responded with new loan products with promises of benefiting both borrowers and investors through the home equity in America.

Borrowers were led to believe that home values were much higher than they had previously thought. This notion was originated by Wall Street firms and was eventually supported throughout the banking industry. Lenders were offering low-interest **H**ome **E**quity **L**ines **O**f

Credit (commonly referred to as "HELOCs") to homeowners based on "perceived" increase in value of their home. They were advised not to worry because their home values and earnings would outpace their debt before their HELOC's would mature. Lenders and mortgage brokers would receive "significant" fees that were often rolled into the financing so that the borrower would have little to no "out of pocket" expense to close the loan. The American public was encouraged to upgrade their homes and make major purchases with money from their HELOC.

Retailers followed suit by offering financing terms that would delay any payment for up to two years for certain durable goods, like home furnishings. Wall Street lenders facilitated the financing for these purchases and sold the notes to investors as securities.

Investors were led to believe that they would be able to own a part of the home equity wealth in America through acquisition of "mortgage-backed securities" and other types of "bundled assets" containing a variety of notes and mortgages of all kinds. As it turned out, these bundled assets were so complicated that they were nearly impossible to place true market value on them. These assets were purchased and held by Investors of all kinds from around the world. Many governments and pension funds participated in this unregulated investment environment. Many investors relied heavily on the expertise and judgment of fund managers to understand the valuation of these assets and protect their interest. Many large investors like Institutions and governments sought the safety of default insurance policies on their investments from insurance giants like AIG. Former members of the Fed and prominent figures in the U.S. financial sector, like Bernard "Bernie" Madoff, endorsed and promoted these financial endeavors.

Everything was built upon the premise of a growing global economy that would eventually "cool-down" and "level-off".

Investors from around the world, particularly those with currency having an exchange rate higher than the dollar, began to purchase these securities at an alarming rate in a rush to own a piece of the U.S. mortgage market at what seemed to be a discount. Top Economic advisors warned that there was an economic bubble being created due to what the chairman of the Federal Reserve, Allen Greenspan, described as "irrational exuberance".

THE RECESSION OF 2008

In 2008, the U.S. economy went into a recession that was greatly attributed to an overvalued and over-leveraged U.S. housing market. Millions of American citizens began to lose their homes and their jobs due to a plunge in spending which caused the marketplace economy to shrink.

The Dow Jones Industrial Average rose by over 30% within 3 years, which was unprecedented. All earning records were broken in virtually every industry, especially the financial sector. In July 2007, the Dow closed above the 14,000 mark, peaking in October 2007 at 14,164.53. The price of fuel skyrocketed. Investors began to pull out of the stock market as the housing bubble popped. On September 28th 2008, the Dow fell 777 points, which was a loss of 7%. This was the biggest one day loss in the history of the Dow (by points, not percentage). On February 27th 2009, the Dow closed at 7,062, having lost more than 50% of its October 2007 high.

THE MILLENNIAL WEALTH EXCHANGE PART-2: THE BANK BAILOUT (TARP)

By 2008, the banking system, along with major Wall Street Investment firms began to falter. The era of "irrational exuberance" had come to an end. The U.S. federal government, along with the Federal Reserve, began the long and painful process of financial bail outs. Initial efforts were focused on shoring up the banking system. In late 2008, the banks started to receive hundreds of billions in taxpayer dollars. This effort was called the federal "stimulus package". The American people were lead to believe that these funds would be used to stem off waves of foreclosures and provide new jobs.

As a tremendous shock to the American people, AIG, one of the world's largest insurance companies, announced that it was on the verge of collapse. AIG had reportedly issued a large number of credit-default swaps (CDS), which were essentially insurance contracts on securities. AIG guaranteed the value of securities that were deemed as virtually "risk-free". By the end of 2007, AIG was holding close to $61 billion in policies with exposure to subprime mortgages, which were at the root of the economic crisis. Among the policy holders were Banks (international and domestic), pension funds, local governments and foreign investors from around the world.

In an unprecedented move by the U.S. government, led by the Treasury Department, AIG was given a large portion of the stimulus funds in concert with the banks and select Wall Street firms deemed as "To Big to fail." When AIG was granted bailout funds, the policy holders were paid, including U.S. banks.

Within a matter of months, many major U.S. banks that received bailout funds moved toward returning the funds to the US government, as they had recovered much of their losses through insurance claims. Once the bailout funds are returned, banks have no obligation to participate in the stimulus plan via lending to small businesses and financing consumer products. "Preservation of Wealth" is the focus of most banks during a recession. Banks are obligated to their shareholders first and foremost.

While millions of American families lost their homes and their wealth, many of those who were primarily responsible for the housing bubble retained the enormous profits that were produced by the bubble. To add insult to injury, many of these policies called for payment to the insured for a cash amount equal to the appraised "lost value" of the asset while retaining ownership of the devalued asset. In other words, the insured get to keep ownership or control of the properties, putting them in the position to wait the market out and profit yet again when the time is right.

> *"Unless the mass retains sufficient control over those entrusted with the powers of their government, these will be perverted to their own oppression, and to the perpetuation of wealth and power in the individuals and their families selected for the trust. Whether our Constitution has hit on the exact degree of control necessary, is yet under experiment." -Thomas Jefferson to M. van der Kemp, 1812.*

Essentially, a dramatic transfer of wealth had taken place, funded in large by average American homeowners and taxpayers. American homeowners leveraged their greatest assets, their homes, for the promise of a higher standard of living and higher home values in the future. The promise turned out to be false, resulting in many Americans losing their jobs, their homes, their wealth, their security and their hope for the future.

Nonetheless, the taxpayers were coerced by a majority Democratic congress into securing the wealth of the market through the government bailout program, particularly with AIG.

TECHNOLOGICAL EVENTS: 2000 - 2008

There were a number of milestones in technology that took place during this period of time, including, but not limited to:

- Voice Over Internet Protocol (VOIP) becomes popular
- Flat screen LCD and Plasma TV's & monitors become affordable
- Google takes over the internet search engine market
- Cell phones with internet access were introduced by Nokia

- Facebook was founded in 2004
- Julian Assange founded Wiki-Leaks in 2005
- Apple introduces the I-Phone in 2007

POLITICAL EVENTS: 2000-2008

Among the notable events in U.S. politics that took place throughout the2000's, they include:

- President Bush selects Retired General Colin Powell as Secretary of State 2000 - 2004.
- President Bush selects Condoleezza Rice to replace outgoing Retired General Colin Powell as Secretary of State 2004 - 2008.
- President Bush is accused of collusion with Blackwater USA in providing exclusive defense contracts that employed private contractor soldiers as support to the troops in Iraq
- Vice-president Dick Cheney is accused of collusion with the Halliburton Corporation in providing exclusive defense contracts for infrastructure support services to the troops in Iraq
- Secretary of Defense Donald Rumsfeld is accused of mishandling the troop deployment in Iraq against the advice from the Secretary of State and former Chairman of the U.S. Joint Chiefs of staff General Colin Powell
- U.S. soldiers are accused of torturing prisoners being detained at Abu Grebe Prison in Iraq and Guantanamo Bay Prison in Cuba.

[page left blank]

CHAPTER IX

THE OBAMA YEARS 2008 – 2016 [D]

AMERICA'S HOPE FOR RECOVERY

In January 2009, Democratic President Barack Hussein Obama, with his vice-president Joseph Biden, took office along with a Democratic majority in congress. They defeated their Republican rivals, being a U.S. Senator from Arizona, John McCain and his running mate, the Governor of Alaska, Sarah Palin. Obama ran his campaign on the premise of bringing change to Washington D.C. and the failed fiscal policies of the Bush administration.

The Obama campaign was able to successfully exploit the weaknesses of the Republican Party by attracting Ultra-Liberal and Moderate voters with promises of social and fiscal policy reforms throughout government. Consequently, matters relating to the Economy, Healthcare and Unemployment became the Obama administration's primary focus. Government spending soared to new heights, increasing the federal trade deficit "juggernaut" to unprecedented and historical levels while unemployment continued to climb nationwide. By the beginning of 2009, all economic trends were in reverse from the end of the Clinton years and the early part of the decade prior to September 11th, 2001.

- ⇩Home sales are down
- ⇩Consumer spending is down
- ⇧Unemployment is up
- ⇧Household savings are on the rise
- ⇧Fuel and Food prices are up

These trends are expected to continue for some time, eventually leading to inflation (devaluation of currency).

President Obama's first term of office would be primarily focused on responding to the ongoing threats of terrorism and a failed U.S. economy.

THE WAR ON AL-QAEDA

Since taking office in 2008, President Obama has narrowed the war on terrorism to the U.S. being at war with al-Qaeda. Since the start of the Invasion on Iraq, Al-Qaeda has grown into multiple groups with various divisions each having their own unique identity. However, Al-Qaeda is unified by its negative sentiments against the U.S. and Israel. They also have a common bond of loyalty to one leader, Osama Bin-Laden. In May of 2011, Bi-Laden was "allegedly" killed in Pakistan by U.S. Special Forces, bringing an end to the most intense international manhunt in history, lasting for 10 years.

OBAMA'S SECOND TERM AS PRESIDENT

With the reported capture and killing of Osama Bin-Laden and the economy showing apparent signs of strengthening, President Obama would spend his second term focusing on keeping his campaign promises to the LGBT community along with national healthcare and issues related to social justice in America. He would also focus on expanding his global influence through greater participation in unified global initiatives like NATO and the United Nations while supporting regime change in Middle-Eastern Arab countries ruled by dictators.

GAY RIGHTS

President Obama accomplished more for Gay rights in his second term than any other American President before him.

- Same-sex marriage law passed with equal protection clause guarantees same-sex marriage in all 50 states.
- Repeal of Defense Of Marriage Act (DOMA).
- Adoption rights for same-sex couples.
- LGBT personnel are allowed to serve openly in the U.S. military.
- Transgender declassified as an illness.
- Transgender public restroom usage rights granted.

BLACK LIVES MATTER MOVEMENT

As the nation's first Black President, Barak Obama was often characterized by the African-American community as not being "black-enough" with regards to issues of racial equality in America. However, during his second-term of office, he became an outspoken supporter of the Black Lives Matter movement. This organization was brought into existence by what seemed to be systemic unjustified police brutality against people of color, (particularly black males) that often led to fatalities. The group was founded in 2013 after the acquittal of George Zimmerman who fatally shot an unarmed African-American teen named Travon Martin as an armed citizen on neighborhood watch patrol. Within a year's time there were a number of black men and women brutalized and killed on what seemed like a regular basis by Law Enforcement Officers in cities around the country. The Black Lives Matter group staged protests around the country in response to the killings. President Obama expressed support for the group and admonished Police Agencies for their role in the wrongful treatment of Black people. This issue was widely debated and divisive among the American people as it drove a wedge between supporting Police Officers and the lives of Black people.

POISED FOR WORLD LEADERSHIP

U.S. presidents have traditionally taken a posture of sovereignty from most unified global initiatives, particularly those that were not viewed as being in the best interest of the U.S. simply for the sake of global common globally. Leading the world from the fringes rather than submitting to global government restrictions.

President Obama has taken on many global agenda initiatives that have expanded his influence well beyond U.S. borders toward becoming a world leader that will likely extend beyond his presidency. He has taken leadership roles in NATO and the United Nations that are unprecedented supporting global initiatives that are controversial in the U.S. and seen as detrimental to our nation's sovereignty.

- Established the Global Agricultural and Food Security Program (GAFSP) in 2009.
- Launched the Global Health Security Agenda (GHSA).
- Launched the Power Africa initiatives geared toward increasing access to power for Sub-Saharan African nations.
- Established the U.S. Global Development Policy in 2010.
- Established the Global Development Council in 2012.
- Supports the Global Climate Change Initiative.
- Supports the Trans Pacific Partnership Agreement (TPP).

TECHNOLOGICAL EVENTS: 2009 - 2016

There were a number of milestones in technology that took place during this period of time, including, but not limited to:

- Google introduces the Droid mobile phone to compete with Apple's I-phone.
- The Cloud computer server system is introduced to the public.
- NASA decommissions the Space Shuttle program.

POLITICAL EVENTS: 2009 - 2016

There were a number of notable events in U.S. politics that took place during this period of time, including, but not limited to:

- Conflict between President Obama and the Congress over raising the Federal debt ceiling to stimulate the failing U.S. economy.
- The Affordable Care Act (ACA) also known as "Obama Care" became law in 2010 and was upheld by the Supreme Court in 2012.
- Planned Parenthood employees secretly filmed selling organs harvested from aborted babies in a nonchalant manner in 2011.
- President Obama signs Executive Order removing restrictions on Federal funding for embryonic stem cell research.
- NSA Contractor Edward Snowden reveals classified U.S. government documents to journalists at The Guardian and The Washington Post newspapers that were made public.
- Troop withdrawal from Iraq took place.
- Arab Spring: Regime change in Egypt and Libya.
- The Islamic State in Iraq and Syria (ISIS) is established.

- ISIS invades Syria and wages war against the government.
- Libyan rebels attack the U.S. Embassy in Bin Ghazi killing the U.S. Ambassador.
- President Obama supports the Iranian Nuclear Deal.
- Conservative Supreme Court Justice Antonin Scalia's sudden and mysterious death in 2016.
- Black Lives Matter Movement was founded in 2013.
- Same-Sex Marriage law was upheld by the Supreme Court in 2015.

[page left blank]

CHAPTER X

THE BROKEN MONETARY SYSTEM

THE BANKING DILEMMA

Over the past couple of decades, conventional banking has dramatically changed its focus and strategies toward dealing with depositors. Commerce and Industry in the U.S., along with most other developed countries, have become reliant on banks to maintain the flow of capital that allows them to operate. Small businesses without large cash reserves are most dependent on the availability of capital from banks through loans and lines of credit.

In theory, the basic flow of revenue typically begins with deposits. Bank depositors have a variety of profiles from working class people typically seeking to manage their funds in an organized and accountable way to investors (private and institutional) seeking to increase and protect their wealth. Banks provide a number of money management services designed to reap a profit from each depositor in some form or fashion.

Traditionally, banks have relied heavily on their ability to make loans to "credit worthy" people or businesses that have adequately displayed earning potential and the ability to repay the loan with interest. Most borrowers are required to provide a certain amount of collateral that is commiserate to the level of risk or exposure to loss taken on by the bank. Ideally, the loan is made from the bank to the borrower. A payment schedule is established for repayment of the principle and interest per agreement. Interest payments represent the bulk of the payments being made in the first portion of the loan's term. The bank's intent is to reap the profits as quickly as possible on the front end while relying on the collateral to cover potential defaults on the back end. This practice is designed to ensure the integrity of the banking system.

THE LENDING FREEZE

If loans are made to borrowers that do not display earning potential or the ability to repay along with the absence of adequate collateral that will mitigate the risk and exposure to loss, the integrity of the banking system would eventually become compromised. In a recession, especially like the one in 2008 caused by devaluation of the housing market, it becomes extremely difficult for banks to make loans due to the high level of risk and exposure to loss.

Gold was replaced with equity and hard assets as the common measure of wealth in the U.S. As a result, home equity became one of the largest equity-asset in the country. Because housing is a fundamental need for everyone, when the value of home equity assets abruptly fell, it brought into question the value of everything else, including goods and services. This is the reason why banks are reluctant to make loans of any kind that are not "fully" collateralized. Until "the bottom" is established, (the true value of homes) values can't be accurately appraised. The true bottom will be found when a balance between earnings and home prices is re-established.

THE RESTRUCTURING OF BANKING

Until such time that home values are "clearly" re-established, banks seem to have adjusted their focus on other ways to generate revenue. Many have turned to higher fees. Some banks seem to have become "fee-based" as their business model. Unfortunately, fees target those who are least able to afford them. It is commonly known that people who are living from paycheck to paycheck often encounter situations that lead to transactions that result in Non-Sufficient Funds (NSF) or cause their bank account to become overdrawn. New customers are offered free checking accounts and encouraged to sign up for Overdraft Protection (OP). If used, OP comes with a hefty fee, regardless to the amount of the overdraft. There are even times when an account will be charged NSF and Returned Check fees as a result of one transaction. The average fee is about $35.00 per occurrence.

Independent Payday lenders are in many cases the lesser of two evils with regards to dealing with short term loans for people with unbalanced budgets leading to financial shortfalls. If the bank would set criteria and allow checking accounts to be overdrawn to a certain dollar amount "known" to the customer for a set penalty fee, they would be providing the same service as payday lenders. Banks would have an advantage over independent payday lenders because their infrastructure is superior and more convenient for its customers. However, some independent payday lenders, along with the retail giant Wal-Mart, are competing with institutional banks by obtaining bank status and building infrastructure. As a result, banks will eventually be forced to adjust its fee policies as its working class depositors opt to do business with their competitors offering more "sensible" shortfall payday loan fees.

This reality has been recently been evidenced by the wireless communications giants being forced to compete with upstart companies. New companies have an advantage by providing a "good" service at an "affordable" rate with a "reasonable" return on their investment. Larger companies typically have more experience, vast infrastructure and provide better service. However, these attributes no longer equate into justification for higher rates in the minds of many modern consumers. Technology and freedom of information has made it possible for an upstart to quickly compete with the institutional giants of days past.

Like many companies doing business on the internet, banks are taking advantage of building client profile data bases for future marketing opportunities. Many banks offer a number of bill pay services and personal money management applications to their customers using the internet banking services. They have rightly calculated that internet banking will become the primary means of banking in the near future, therefore they are preparing for it now. Banking is no different than any other business in the sense that they are looking ahead to the future and doing whatever they believe is necessary to protect themselves and the interest of their clients, being the investors and depositors.

THE KEY ROLE OF THE CENTRAL BANK

THE FED AND THE U.S. TREASURY

In the U.S., free market private banks have traditionally been used as the standard financial interface between the general public and the U.S. treasury through a central bank known as The Federal Reserve Bank (a.k.a. "The Fed"). Here are some basic facts about the Federal Reserve Bank and the U.S. Treasury with regards to the U.S. monetary system:

1. The Fed is a conglomerate of private banking institutions and is not a branch of the of the U.S. Government
2. The Fed is made up of 12 regional banks:
    - Boston, New York, Philadelphia, Cleveland, Richmond, Atlanta, Chicago, St. Louis, Minneapolis, Kansas City, Dallas and San Francisco
    - There are 25 branches nationwide
3. The Fed is the central bank of the U.S. Government.
4. The Fed also provides services to other banks and investors
5. The U.S. Government is a client to the Fed just like people and businesses are clients to their local banking institutions

6. The Fed provides the U.S. Government with various financial services, including:
    - Handling U.S. Treasury's payments
    - Selling government securities
    - Assisting the U.S. Treasury with cash management and investments
    - Providing the U.S. Treasury with Emergency loans, Operating Capital & Lines of Credit
7. The Fed charges the U.S. Government interest and fees for its services much like any other bank would
8. The Fed is a sovereign corporate entity led by a Board of Governors and its Chairman.
9. The Fed is controlled by various stockholders (known and unknown to the public).
10. Terms for collateral, interest and loan repayment are determined by high-ranking representatives of the U.S. Treasury and the Fed.
11. U.S. currency is a note from the Fed.
    - In essence, U.S. dollars are like personalized "cashier checks" that are printed for the U.S. government to pay its debt obligations

12. The U.S. Treasury is insolvent.
    - Deposits to the U.S. Treasury that are capable of backing the U.S. government's debt and the face value of currency have not been maintained for decades
13. U.S. currency notes can no longer be used to redeem its value in precious metals (like gold and silver) from the U.S. Treasury, which has been the common practice of most governments that have used collateralized currency systems for centuries.

14. Each Silver Certificate stated that there was a deposit in the U.S. Treasury that substantiated the value of this official legal tender. Furthermore, the certificate insured the bearer's entitlement to its value in silver on demand.

The last delivery of $1 Silver Certificates was made in November of 1963. In March 1964, Secretary of Treasury Dillon halted the redemption of Silver Certificates in silver dollars and on 24 Jun 1968, redemption in silver bullion was discontinued.

CONTROL OF THE ECONOMY

It seems that the U.S. government has relinquished control of its monetary policies to the Fed. In the current climate of global economic uncertainty and bank failures, why does the U.S. government have all of its "fiscal eggs" in the Federal Reserve Bank "basket?" The answer to this question begins with knowing who controls the Fed and being able to determine who benefits from its actions. You must also understand where the modern western society is inevitably heading in order to comprehend the motivation behind what seems to be failed fiscal policies on the surface.

Things that don't make sense today make perfect sense when viewed through the perspective of those who are shaping the world's future. Whether you are a follower of so-called "conspiracy theories" that lead you to the agendas of "secret societies" and their quest for world domination or a Christian that believes what Jesus said about this age, all roads lead to the same conclusion. Specific knowledge about world events is simply a tool to forecast events in the near future like a barometer is used to forecast the weather. In both cases, the purpose is to make preparations before the event takes place.

[Matthew 24:3-31]

CONTROL OF THE FED

U.S. monetary policy is shaped by the Fed. The Fed is fully controlled by Jewish and European interest. Historically speaking, common Jewish geo-political interest has included, establishing economic control and survival of their national heritage, which has worked hand-in-hand for them throughout generations. Many European countries have historically pursued agendas including conquest and promotion of ethnic superiority. Economic control within the most powerful nation on the planet becomes an essential position for Jews in a world that is rapidly becoming more pro-Islamic.

However, with the rapid decline of the U.S. economy and its loss of controlling influence around the world, Fed stockholders would be wise to leverage their control over the U.S. monetary system toward European economies before the U.S. collapse. In fact, with globalization being inevitable, one might think that the U.S. economic demise was engineered by those with controlling interest of the Fed in preparation for the transition. The U.S. bank bailout of 2008 is a prime example of such posturing.

Facts regarding control of the Federal Reserve Bank:

- Jews control 8 out of the 12 Reserve banks
- Jews hold a majority on the Fed Board of Governors
- Europeans make up the majority of the remaining Fed leadership

Jews significantly influence many aspects of the U.S. economy, politics and society as a whole through control over the media industry and banking. The U.S., having Christian roots, military superiority and geopolitical influence in the middle-east and throughout world, continues to protect the nation of Israel from annihilation by its Muslim neighbors. The future of Israel as a sovereign Jewish state will be at risk if the U.S. ceases to support Israeli policies regarding the Palestinians.

THE NEW GLOBAL STANDARD OF WEALTH

THE GOLD AND SILVER PARADIGM

Gold and silver have been historically and traditionally recognized as the standard of wealth commonly used and accepted as collateral for currency by kingdoms and governments around the world. Gold has been revered for the purity of its composition and its durability and beauty. Silver has been revered for its durability and versatility of use, particularly as currency coins. I believe that we have reached a place in history where the role and value of gold and silver shall dramatically change.

Younger generations do not have the same appreciation for gold and silver beyond their practical and industrial uses. As the mainstream monetary system becomes fully electronic, the practical value of gold and silver will plummet along with its worth. In the meantime, assets that are traditionally secure in the west, which include gold, silver and housing, are subject to value manipulation based on influenced perception and historical precedence. As a result, great wealth will be shifted from the common investors, ultimately, into the hands of those who are preparing for the future of "Technology-Based" Assets.

DEPENDENCY ON TECHNOLOGY

In the name of progress, we have become a global society that is dependent on western technology for every aspect of life. Some of the categories affected include:

1. Housing
2. Food and Water Supply
3. Clothing
4. Productivity
5. Transportation
6. Communication
7. Entertainment / Social Media

We depend on advanced equipment and manufacturing to produce the tools and equipment necessary to build our homes, process and package our foods and make our clothing. The workplace depends on computers and high-tech machinery for high-output productivity with accuracy. Civilization depends on the modern transportation system for providing domestic commutes and travel abroad to the general public along with delivery of goods worldwide. Our modern civil infrastructure is built on electronic communications. Entertainment and social networking is becoming synonymous with electronic media for younger generations.

In theory, technology can continue to function without fossil fuels and with limited precious metals being used. However, the modern world cannot function in a progressive manner without modern technology. A major disruption to the power grid and communications system would catapult a modern society into complete chaos overnight. Control of this commodity is indeed possession of the most powerful resource in the world system. **Technology Based Assets** is the new global standard of wealth.

KEY INVENTIONS

The discovery of electricity was the catalyst that launched a new era for mankind. There are (7) key inventions that have paved the way for modern technology:

1. Printing press
2. Camera
3. Telephone
4. Phonograph
5. Film projector
6. Radio
7. Television

These (7) key inventions have become indispensable technologies in today's world. They are individually referred to as forms of media and collectively called multi-media. Computers have been used to modernize and expand the common use and access to multi-media technologies. These key inventions have evolved into:

1. Portable Digital File
2. Digital Camera
3. Wireless Communication
4. Micro chip
5. Multi-dimensional Holographic projection
6. Digital Satellite audio
7. Digital Streaming video

Access to multi-media technology has become focused on Personal Electronic Devices. Distribution of media has become merged through the internet. Technologies that use to require several devices can now be accessed through a single hand-held device.

THE CLOUD: ELECTRONIC INFORMATION MANAGEMENT SYSTEM

Ultimately, all access and distribution of all media content will become centralized. The process of media centralization is referred to as Cloud computing or simply "The Cloud". The Cloud is an electronic information management system originally designed to store and control the flow of all media content. The stored and controlled content on the Cloud shall include:

- Official Records
- Personal Information and Media
- Medical Records
- Banking Information
- Personal Software Subscriptions
- Navigation & Travel Records
- Real-Time Satellite Location

The Cloud will ultimately replace all systems that utilize any form of plastic cards for transactions or identification. Personal Electronic Devices will initially be the most commonly used means for the general public gaining access to the Cloud. Access codes and passwords will eventually be phased out by some form of electronic implant or mark (like a barcode) on each subscriber.

Some of the alleged benefits to using the Cloud that will be promoted include:

1. No risk of computer viruses or Hackers
2. No risk of identity theft
3. No software malfunctions due to missing updates

4. No lost data problems
5. No more cash or plastic cards to keep up with
6. Constant access to all forms of media 24/7 365 days
7. Convenience

In an electronic world, the Cloud system is "undoubtedly" the ultimate solution to data, information access and distribution. However, the Cloud will effectively end an era marked by Freedom of Information and Personal Privacy being considered as basic rights for common citizens in western civilization. Privacy will be a thing of the past and media will be fully controlled, tightly monitored and distributed only to subscribers that agree to the terms of use called the End User License Agreement (commonly referred to as the EULA agreement). People will no longer have to wonder about who has access to their personal information. The Cloud will ultimately allow government and their approved agents to have full access and control over all electronic information and content.

[page left blank]

CHAPTER XI

TRANSITIONING TO THE "NEW NORMAL" 2012 – 2016

MESSAGE OF HOPE FADES – AMERICA IS IN "SURVIVAL-MODE"

Leading economists from around the world all agree that recovery from this recession will be slow. Most predict a 7 to 10 year cycle of economic recovery. There is also a widespread consensus among leading economist that the U.S. will not return to its former stature of being the world economic leader. The 2008 U.S. recession is often compared to the most recent Japanese recession that has lasted for 10 to 20 years depending on varying opinions regarding when it actually began. As a result, consumer spending will decrease while household savings will increase. However, the value of currency will decline due to inflation caused by the reduction in spending. Currency devaluation offsets any hope for immediate asset gains on increased household savings. This vicious cycle will have broad and dramatic rippling affects throughout the U.S. and western civilization as a whole.

All indications point to the European Union (EU) and China emerging as the new world economic leaders. The EU brings governance and leadership while China provides vast resources and a growing consumer base capable of eventually replacing the U.S. as the world's leading source of consumption. Even if the U.S. returns to a form of economic vibrancy and vitality, things like social morality, rights to privacy and the sovereignty of a Christian nation are not likely to ever return to this country. America, along with the rest of the Western society, has become enslaved to its worldly passions and the conveniences of modern technology. As a result, there will be relatively little opposition to the dramatic changes in economic policies taking place, which will lead us into the third and final part of the millennial wealth exchange.

The first part of the millennial wealth exchange was the pinnacle of how capitalism works and its lasting effects on society. The housing bubble crisis fueled by sub-prime lending showed the nature of dream makers (primarily lenders in this case) and dreamers

(Primarily home owners) with clear winners and losers on display. The second part of the millennial wealth exchange illustrated the far-reaching power of the dream makers (a.k.a. ruling class) who forced the U.S. government to ensure delivery of their plunder from the American economy by providing a government bailout to the banking system that was funded by U.S. taxpayers. AIG was a major instrument in this process as they provided insurance policies designed to mitigate the risk of sub-prime investments made by many of the world's largest banks. AIG defaulted and the taxpayers were forced to bail them out under the auspices of being "too big to fail". The loss claims were paid and the banks were made whole through AIG while many American taxpayers experienced a significant loss of wealth from the dramatic drop in home values. The third and final part of the millennial wealth exchange will take place in the midst of the global economic system being restructured through tax reform and debt collection policy reform. This final stage will set the new world economic standards and firmly secure the place of the ruling class. At this point, dreamers will stop dreaming and dream makers will become nightmares to those that are indebted to them.

THE MILLENNIAL WEALTH EXCHANGE PART-3: TAXES AND DEBT COLLECTION

TAX REFORM

There has been an ongoing debate in the country regarding taxation since the founding of this nation. The original British colonies in America sought and gained Independence from Great Brittan primarily due to disputes over tax policies.

Some of the most contentious tax issues include:

- Income Tax vs. Flat Tax
- Higher Taxes on the Wealthy
- Tax Loop Holes
- Corporate Tax Incentives

- Tax Exemptions and Credits

The economic system failure will necessitate a dramatic overhaul to the tax system. The all-encompassing information management system known as "The Cloud" will present the opportunity for tax equity. Once a policy is established, assessments and collections will be governed and regulated by virtually infallible Artificial Intelligence instead of Bureaucrats and government employees. The efficiency of the cloud will make up for all budget shortfalls and provide reliable economic data which will eliminate any potential for future system collapse. Millions of Americans supplement their income with earnings that are paid "under the table", which has historically been out of reach from taxation. This type of transaction will no longer be possible in a fully electronic monetary system that closes all such loop holes. People will be forced to live with whatever is left after taxes are consistently, automatically and instantly deducted immediately after earnings are electronically posted.

DEBT COLLECTION POLICY REFORM

Americans have become accustom to lifestyles that include having outstanding debt as a fundamental component. Our society encourages long term debt, (like 30 year home mortgages) and renewable debt (like car loans every 3 – 5 years and revolving credit accounts) that have become the foundation of our financial markets.

However, as a result of the failed economy, many of these debt obligations are ending in default. Government has attempted to stimulate the economy through providing default guarantees to the largest financial market investors citing that this action would prompt lenders to increase investments and loans to small business which would bring new jobs and ultimately bring about renewed consumer spending. Instead, the financial markets decided to sit on their assets and wait for economic uncertainty to dissipate. As a result, the markets continue to destabilize from increasing national debts, loss of jobs and individual wealth through falling 401k and retirement accounts.

In order to restore confidence to the financial markets, new debt collection policies must go into effect. The cloud information management system will be employed to manage all debt collection electronically. This action will dramatically decrease the possibility of total debt default. The opportunity for debt forgiveness through bankruptcy will be dramatically diminished, opting toward lifetime indebtedness that is enforceable worldwide. People will be forced to live with whatever is left after debt payments are consistently, automatically and instantly deducted immediately after earnings are electronically posted. This policy will extend to other forms of debt, including:

Court Ordered Debt

- Civil Judgments & Liens
- Penalties & Fines
- Spousal or Child Support

Government Loans

- Student Loans
- HUD Loans
- SBA Loans

Healthcare Coverage

- Hospital Bills
- Prescription Drug Expenses

This ultimate system of tax and debt collection will be virtually "indisputable" due to the failed condition of the economy and the equitable oversight and application provided by the cloud information management system. The alternative would be to have an unstable economic system that would ultimately lead to the breakdown of civil society and increased global mayhem.

These changes will trigger an exchange of wealth and power on an institutional level. These policy revisions will essentially change what was formerly 'risky" consumer debt to an arrangement that forces the borrower to become "indentured" to the lender until the debt is paid in full. Financial markets will become fully confident as they acquire control over the performance of their financial investments and future projections.

NEW COMMUNITY STANDARDS IN THE U.S. AND ABROAD

RELIGION

- THE END OF JUDEO-CHRISTIAN MORALITY AS THE FOUNDATION OF OUR CIVILIZATION
- CATHOLICISM & ISLAM DOMINATE ALL OTHER FORMS OF WORLD RELIGION
- ONE-WORLD RELIGION ENCAPSULATES ALL SYSTEMS OF BELIEF EXCEPT TRUE CHRIST FOLLOWERS

GAY RIGHTS (LGBT)

- SAME-SEX MARRIAGE SETS A STANDARD FOR THE MODERN FAMILY
- GAYS CULTURE PERMEATES THE MILITARY
- GAY RIGHTS MOVEMENT TAKES PRECEDENCE OVER BLACK CIVIL RIGHTS MOVEMENT

CHILD EMPOWERMENT

- CHILDREN'S RIGHTS TAKE PRECEDENCE OVER PARENTS RIGHTS
- CHILDREN LEGAL GAIN RIGHTS TO PRIVACY FROM THEIR PARENTS

WOMEN IN LEADERSHIP

- WOMEN POLITICAL LEADERS AND CORPORATE EXECUTIVES SHALL BE THE STANDARD RATHER THAN THE EXCEPTION
- WOMEN AS FAMILY BREAD WINNERS WILL BE CONSIDERED AS NORMAL BY THE CULTURE

CHAPTER XII

"THE NEW NORMAL"
2017 – 2020

The incoming president and his administration will be tasked with getting the country settled into accepting the reality of a new normal. Ultimately, the essential U.S. Government infrastructure budgets and entitlement programs, along with new fiscal policies and standards, will be used as a statistical platform for private industry to build sustainable lifestyle initiatives that seamlessly interface with government initiatives.

RESTRUCTURED RESIDENTIAL COMMUNITIES AND TRENDS

Suburban and rural communities will become more segregated due to many polarizing socio-economic factors. Many will choose to live in communities with like-minded neighbors, regardless of their financial wherewithal, in order to participate in their culture of choice.

However, urban population centers will experience the opposite effect. Their common bond will be the desire for staying connected to the world and the sense of "peace and safety" associated with being where businesses and government have committed to providing services into the foreseeable future. All of the world's major resources will be concentrated toward densely populated urban communities and travel corridors that connect them. Living in harmony will be the theme of the day as it is forced upon society by the need for social stability and economic viability.

MORALITY STANDARDS	FAMILY LIFESTYLE STANDARDS
Liberal a) Secular b) Religious c) Non-Secular	***Consumer*** a) Economic Optimist b) Media-Driven c) Retail Shoppers d) Trend Followers

MORALITY STANDARDS	FAMILY LIFESTYLE STANDARDS
Conservative	***Conservative***
a) Religious	a) Economic Realist
b) Non-Religious	b) Reality-Driven
c) Secular	c) Thrift Shoppers
	d) Recyclers

CIRCUMSTANTIAL COMMUNITY DEVELOPMENT

The days of the masses being enticed to live a lifestyle beyond their means shall continue to fade away as reality sets in. Many will be compelled to live in communities that reflect their family's socio-economic condition for a number of reasons. Consumers will continue to live in the hope for a resurgence of free market capitalism thinking that "waiting it out" is the way to go. In the meantime, they will continue to follow the markets and ride the daily financial reports rollercoaster until it completely derails. Those who are conservative-minded will adapt their lifestyles to what seems to be rational based on the facts of their circumstances. They will "make-do" with what they have and learn to maximize their resources.

SUBURBAN GHETTOS

Since the 1980's, there has been prolific suburban community development. Government has struggled to provide adequate levels of service to these communities due to the high-cost of infrastructure, maintenance and personnel requirements. Such services include: fire rescue, law enforcement, utilities (water, sewer, storm water), roads, etc. Suburban communities will continue to experience the flight of homeowners seeking to obtain a secure investment with a more stable environment and predictable outlook. As a result, suburban ghettos will emerge and encroach on the residents of communities that were designed for middle class homeowners. As home values plummet, renters from all social and financial backgrounds will replace former homeowners.

HOMEOWNERSHIP

The posture of homeownership can be placed into four general categories that I'd like to refer to as being Blessed, Privileged, Disadvantaged and At-Risk. There will be few buyers of new single-family homes as multi-family residential development is the most economically feasible way for government to manage public resources and services. In fact, many single-family homes will become (or be used as) multi-family dwellings. The following are conditions that characterize each category of homeowner.

BLESSED

<u>Owners of "modest" homes</u>

- no mortgage having significant equity
- having "cash on hand" equal to 3-years or more modest living expenses
- having a reliable source of self-produced income from providing essential goods and/or services
- having land that supports a private well for water and a septic system in an environmentally sound location (preferably rural)
- having renewable energy back-up systems (like solar and wind)
- having wood-burning source of home heating and cooking

PRIVILEGED

<u>Owners of "modest" homes</u>

- having a small mortgage with significant equity

- having "cash on hand" equal to at least 1-year modest living expenses
- having a primary source of income from a thriving industry
- having a private well for water and a septic system or at least water and sewer services provided by a municipality
- having energy efficient appliances
- having wood-burning source of home heating and cooking

DISADVANTAGED

Owners of "modest" homes

- having a sizeable mortgage with little or no equity
- having "cash on hand" equal to less than 1-year modest living expenses
- having a primary source of income from a "shrinking" industry
- having water and sewer services provided by a private contractor
- having standard electric and gas sources of home heating and cooking w/ no back-up power supply system

AT-RISK

Owners of "large or inefficient" homes

- having a sizeable mortgage with negative equity
- having little to no "cash on hand"
- having significant consumer debt and loans
- having an "unreliable" source of income

- having well water and a septic system in an environmentally "unstable" location (i.e. ground water contamination or flood zone)
- having standard electric and gas sources of home heating and cooking

NEW HOUSING STANDARDS

Pre-existing housing will undergo a transformation toward energy efficiency simply to make it economically feasible for people to remain in these homes. New home standards will undergo revolutionary changes to meet the challenges of the new normal. Virtually every aspect of homebuilding will be subject to intense scrutiny resulting in significant modifications or changes within the industry including, but not limited to:

- Interior layout and design (ergonomics)
- Typical space requirements
- Building materials
- Insulation requirements
- Alternative energy compatibility
- Heating and cooling means and methods
- Potable water restriction devices
- Recycled grey water systems
- Wastewater pre-treatment

Home conversions will be backed and subsidized by the federal government and used as another opportunity for economic stimulus. New homes will be primarily multi-family developments providing rental units. Home loans for detached single-family dwellings will be difficult to finance without significant collateralization.

Single-family homes will become most feasible for multi-generational living scenarios. Multi-generational family housing advantages may typically include:

- Multiple contributions to household earnings from employment, pensions, consolidation of assets and other retirement funds
- Active grandparents defraying childcare cost by participating in child-rearing of the younger generation
- Defrayment to cost and "peace of mind" gained by avoiding the need for retirement centers and nursing homes for aging family members
- Overall financial benefits based on the "economy of scales" (volume buying at reduced cost)

TRANSPORTATION

The number of new automobiles being manufactured and purchased will dramatically decline. New fuel standards will begin to phase-out non-compliant vehicles. However, old vehicles will not be replaced on a one to one ratio. Fuel prices will remain high enough to dictate how far they can travel between pay periods for many. Access to an automobile will no longer be taken for granted. It shall be considered a privilege to own one. As a result, mass transit systems will significantly increase. Providing public transportation to business and commerce corridors becomes critical to the economic sustainability of a community. As a result to these factors, there will be a transportation crisis in suburban and rural communities, adding to the pressures on its residents to relocate closer to or within the established service corridors.

GOVERNMENT AND PUBLIC SERVICES

Many U.S. citizens living in or near dense population centers have grown accustom to receiving a number of services being provided by the federal government that are funded by tax revenues. With sharp declines in revenues, government agencies will be forced to augment or discontinue many public services, including but not limited to:

- Parks and recreation facilities
- Public libraries
- Public assistance
    - Unemployment compensation
    - Medicaid
    - Food stamps
- Public works
    - sanitation / trash pick-up
    - transportation / road & right of way maintenance
- Emergency response services
    - fire
    - police
    - animal control

The rising cost of fuel and the growing scarcity of the U.S. water supply will have an extraordinary impact on availability of these vital resources to U.S. households. It is likely that government will tighten regulations in the attempt to make energy and drinking water affordable and accessible. In some cases, it may become necessary for the federal government to nationalize some parts of the energy sector and take control of regional water management districts in order to regulate the distribution. However, the downside to government intervention is that people would become subject to the government's prerogative on the quality and quantity of services being distributed.

RETAIL AND COMMERCE

The buying patterns of households in the U.S. will change dramatically as a result of economic restructuring. The marketplace will reinvent itself based on what is "perceived" as necessary goods and services by the general public. Industry will focus on driving consumer spending toward the superficial and disposable commodities. Electronic devices used for communication and entertainment shall take precedence and become virtually "inseparable" within the lives of average consumers.

As the monetary system becomes fully electronic, brick and mortar establishments and online virtual venues providing goods and services shall become more integrated and uniformed. As a result, the need for brick and mortar retail stores will diminish dramatically. Retailers will focus more on manufacturing, inventory and "cost-effective" direct distribution to customers.

ENTERTAINMENT

There are (5) basic groups targeted by the entertainment industry, being:

1. Infant/Toddler
2. Child
3. Teen/Youth
4. Adult
5. Family

In secular cultures, themes of fantasy, violence and immorality will continue to be used as standards for entertainment. These themes have been found to be the most captivating by mankind and are used as mental coercion tools by mass media providers and government. In modern society, these themes are expressed through all forms of media at every age level, governed by "so-called" rating systems designed to establish and enforce "age appropriate" standards.

Infants and Toddlers are exposed to these themes through seemingly "benign" characters of all kinds presenting themselves as "friendly" and "caring" often in the form of man-made "unidentifiable" creature-like beings. These beings are characterized by their behavior which is often scripted by agenda-driven producers promoting such things as homosexuality and eastern religious philosophies.

Children are further indoctrinated to these themes thorough child-like fantasy and mythical characters like Unicorns, Fairies, Elves and other magical figures. These characters are always presented in a conflict scenario that suggest "good versus evil" thereby defining what is good (trustworthy) and what is evil (adversarial).

This theme continues to build upon itself as children grow into the teens and youth category. The media producers build upon the foundation of fantasy with sorcery, witchcraft and super-human characters. The conflict between good and evil becomes more violent. The scenarios depicted by the conflict suggest that strength ultimately defeats weakness regardless of the moral character being held by either side. Immoral behavior, especially sexual deviancy, becomes promoted as the reward for those who are victorious.

By the time one reaches adulthood, there is a craving for a deeper and "more intense" entertainment experience. A lifetime of media programming and desensitizing leaves adults to seek participation in the highest level of fantasy, violence and immorality that is available. Sanctioned entertainment options are expanded for adults ranging from conventional media to live encounters and interactions involving fantasy, violence and immorality, including all forms of sexual deviancy.

Family entertainment is based on themes deemed appropriate for children and youth embedded with innuendos of adult situations and satire. In this setting, children are exposed to more mature levels while teens and adults settle for mild to moderate levels. Ideally, adults take responsibility for children being exposed to media that is not age appropriate.

The overwhelming majority of entertainment shall be electronic and video related. From personal electronic devices and home entertainment systems to movie theaters and theme parks, interactive gaming, multi-dimensional video and virtual reality experiences shall all be entertainment media standards.

RECREATION

As the global economy continues to become increasingly unstable, recreational habits will be affected. Many factors shall dictate forms of recreation that will be promoted and made readily accessible to the general public. Recreation shall increasingly become more theme-based, categorized, programmatic and electronically controlled.

(5) basic target audiences

1. Infant/Toddler
2. Child
3. Teen / Youth
4. Adult
5. Family

(3) basic recreation categories

1. Indoor
2. Outdoor
3. Home

INDOOR

Theme Parks

Large Theme parks will continue to offer annual passes so that patrons will come and pay for peripheral services like parking, food and souvenirs. Smaller themed venues will follow suit with all-inclusive passes to promote patronage. The price of fuel shall also play a big role in people being able to travel long distances for recreation.

Extracurricular Activities

Participation in traditional indoor activities such as karate, dance, music, etc. will remain popular, but yet diminished by comparable electronic home recreational experiences. Fewer families will be able to afford the cost of memberships and activity fees in their shrinking household budgets. The price of fuel shall also play a big role in people being able to travel longer distances to participate in Intermural sporting events.

Recreational Facilities

Recreation centers shall be adversely affected by budget cuts to operation and maintenance expenses. Reductions in staff will decrease the hours of operation. Some facilities will close altogether to avoid potential liability to government. As a result, private indoor recreation facilities, such as the YMCA and Boys and Girls Club will expand and increase their memberships.

OUTDOOR

Extracurricular Activities

Participation in traditional outdoor activities such as football, baseball, soccer, etc. will become less popular as opportunities to play decrease resulting from budget cuts in the public school system. As a result, private youth sports clubs and leagues will become more popular and shall rival traditional high school sports programs. With the onset of virtual school, public school sports programs may eventually be phased-out altogether and essentially replaced with private youth leagues.

Recreational Facilities

Public parks and beaches shall be adversely affected by cuts to budgets for wildlife and habitat management, facility maintenance, park rangers and lifeguards. Reductions in staff will decrease the hours of operation at all public facilities. Some facilities will close altogether to avoid potential liability to government. Private or Community-owned (and operated) nature parks and beaches will gain popularity. As budget cuts become more necessary, government will be forced to consider leasing some of its best parks to private "for-profit" firms in a similar fashion to its popular Design-Build-Maintain-Operate-Transfer (a.k.a. DBMOT) arrangements for major toll-road projects that are approved but lack government funding.

HOME

Console and Online Gaming

Electronic home entertainment will be the central recreation hub for most families. All electronic industry giants are focused on combining multiple forms of media into one interactive experience that can take place anywhere at any time so long as there is access to the internet. Three dimensional holographic images being projected into the family living room from a multi-media device or total immersion into a 3-D environment online through virtual reality programs will become common. This technology will combine visual and audio affects with social network interaction by allowing people to share the multi-media experiences with others remotely from their individual homes.

This technological advancement will be part of the final evolution toward people becoming captivated with living their lives vicariously through fantasy, fiction or the experiences of others. The broad appeal of multi-user online gaming, like “Farmville”, and reality television, like “American Idol”, are the forerunners to this final step.

MEDIA

Access to the internet will ultimately be available to anyone that chooses to be connected under the terms and conditions required by government. Electronic multi-media devices will be utilized by most people as a safe, fun, convenient and cost-effective means of enjoyment and social interaction. All multi-media devices will offer audio and video content with full graphics. Access to personalized media formats will become synchronized between home, work, school and travel. Every aspect of life will be connected to some form of electronic media for most people.

The widespread use of this multi-media technology will produce a generation where extraordinary gifts, talents and skills are no longer required to participate or excel and be recognized by your peers on a world stage. People will trade in their own identities for chosen identities that are customized for the online world commonly referred to as Avatars.

POPULAR CULTURE AND FASHION

Those who choose to live conservatively and practice modesty must give an effort toward restraint that goes beyond the expression of their natural state of mind or being. However, popular culture and fashion typically follow the trends that reflect the broad consciousness of a society promoted through all forms of media, art and personal expression. The cultural theme of this time will be personal freedom, tolerance, unity and allegiance to the system of oneness. Fashion will be as diverse as the ideas within each society. No form of personal expression will be off-limits or discouraged by society. Open sexuality and homosexuality will continue to be the most popular trendsetting social agendas. Body piercings, tattoos and other physical augmentations for personal aesthetics and identification with specific subcultures will continue to rise in popularity and be accepted as a cultural norm by society.

[Romans 13:12-14, 1 Timothy 2:9-10, 2 Timothy 3:1-7]

EDUCATION

As the global economy continues to become increasingly unstable, educational opportunities and the system as a whole will be dramatically affected. There will continue to be public and private education offered at all levels of learning. However, access to quality education will become more exclusive among the general public. The internet will become the primary venue of general education to the masses for both public and private sectors.

The number of teachers will be "dramatically" reduced in a very short period of time, being replaced in large by Artificial Intelligence computing and software that will ultimately control and administer the online educational system. Human instructional classes shall only be made available to those with special needs and those who can afford to pay for it. However, access to free public education will no longer be considered as an inalienable right to all school-age children. Eventually, parents and children will be required to register and be recognized as a member of the unified global system of government in order to receive public benefits.

(10) basic levels of learning

1. Preschool
2. Primary
3. Secondary
4. Post-Secondary

Trade School

5. Trade & Tech School
6. College
7. Graduate Studies
8. Post-Graduate Studies
9. Doctoral Studies

(3) basic education venues

A. Independent Online Studies
B. Virtual Classroom

Physical Classroom

(3) basic teaching categories

A. Self-Reference
B. Instructional
C. Tutorial

SELF-REFERENCE

It will become increasingly popular for people to seek knowledge on their own through the various forms of public information media. Many professional licensing courses and online educational classes rely heavily on the student's use of reference materials made available by the course provider.

INSTRUCTIONAL AND TUTORIAL

There will be limited free instructional public education made available for a select few based on special circumstances. Direct instructional teaching shall be primarily found in Private school settings. Tutorial education shall follow the same trend as instructional.

EMPLOYMENT

The employment paradigm shall change its basis from "access to information" to "dissemination and interpretation of information". The old paradigm was reliant upon (3) main perceptions:

1. Access to Knowledge
2. Training Requirements
3. High-Risk

OLD EMPLOYMENT PARADIGM

<u>Access to Knowledge:</u>

There was a notion that only a select few of over-achievers would have access to certain information, generally being those who went to college. Access was further buffered by licensing requirements to provide services that paid higher wages.

<u>Training Requirements:</u>

Operation of high-tech equipment and performing technical tasks often required special training. Certification from technical schools was also a requirement for obtaining many of the higher paying jobs.

<u>High-Risk:</u>

It was always understood that there would be jobs that most people would not want to have. Some of these jobs required higher levels of training like law enforcement and Fire rescue. The pay was typically higher because of the higher exposure to hazardous conditions.

Computer technology and access to the internet has redefined the field of employment. The internet has taken us from a society reliant on controlling information access to giving the general public access to "virtually" all information that exists in the world. This factor has leveled the playing field with regards to access and training. Robotics combined with Artificial Intelligence has mitigated many factors that were considered as hazardous to humans. High-risk jobs requiring high-skill levels have been replaced by computer programmers and operators. The new employment paradigm is based on (3) main factors:

1. Actual Knowledge
2. Actual Ability
3. Artificial Intelligence

NEW EMPLOYMENT PARADIGM

Actual Knowledge:

Being able to produce actual work product has outperformed the traditional resume′ as evidence of knowledge. Many useful skills are being acquired by school age youth that are marketable in today's electronic business environment.

Actual Ability

Competency, **C**apability and **C**apacity have outpaced Credentials in today's employment market. True ability to perform at a high level of competency will be required of those with jobs that have not been made obsolete by technology.

Many positions that may have traditionally required someone with years of experience and good judgment are being filled by Artificial Intelligence technology. Companies can program their computers to respond to scenarios in a way that best represents their corporate philosophies.

Artificial Intelligence

Artificial Intelligence and the internet will most dramatically affect the "so-called" middle-class professional on the front end. As a result, pursuit of employment opportunities paying living wages or above will become fiercely competitive as highly educated people begin to step down into lower paying positions. Ultimately, the millions of jobs that are eliminated in the process will have lasting and devastating effects on the least educated population and older workers.

Positions that have traditionally employed people with little education to perform manual labor task, such as sanitation workers or janitors, will be sought after by the displaced well-educated middle-class workers. Positions that were assumed to be better suited for older workers will become filled by younger workers, such as restaurant and retail managers due to the development of computer systems that provides business management and security that can be controlled and monitored remotely that are virtually failsafe. There are a growing number of people becoming a part of the workforce that are completely reliant on computers to perform every task that requires thought. Retail jobs will primarily require that employees are capable of pressing buttons with pictures on electronic devices.

Lower to mid-level management decisions will ultimately be made by machines programmed to respond according company policy. This practice is already being used (in-part) by most major companies in their customer service departments. Very few decision making human beings are deemed as necessary for jobs that required substantial staffing just 20 years ago. Call centers were always hiring due to the sheer volume of calls to answer and the high turnover rate from long, stressful hours. Today, call centers are continually being downsized or shut down around the country. This phenomenon with call center reduction being mentioned is not attributed to outsourcing, which was the main contributing factor throughout the 1980's and 1990's. Human customer service is simply becoming obsolete for most major businesses.

Consumer Technology advocates

Eventually, non-electronic physical transactions will no longer be an option for things like bill paying and account inquiries. As a result, there will briefly be a market for Consumer Technology (CT) advocates. These CT advocates will provide services that assist people who don't know how to get things done electronically. Many self-employed professionals will partake in this industry for a while. There will be a brief bubble of opportunity for Consumer Technology advocates. However, as Artificial Intelligence continues to improve and become more human-like, the need for CT advocates will eventually cease.

RELIGION

There are many thousands of Christian denominations and religious belief systems that have developed over the span of American history. However, in this day of social discord and economic despair, there shall be only (2) main themes of religion that will take precedence. There shall be a world religion that is all-inclusive which will ultimately become the official religion of the unified world government. In contrast, there shall be a remnant from within the mainstream monotheistic religions that hold strongly to their belief in the coming of a messiah.

WORLD RELIGION

As the world continues to unite, religion shall follow the same trend. Leaders from all religions and beliefs shall join together to become the world Church. Everyone shall be urged to be tolerant and respectful of each other's differences. There shall be no condemnation based on moral beliefs and practices. The golden rule theme of this Church shall be tolerance of all moral preferences and mutual respect for all living creatures. A desire for "peace and safety" shall be the motivating factor for many members of the mainstream messianic faiths, including, Christians, Muslims and Jewish leaders, to join this movement.

MESSIANIC BELIEVERS

Those who believe in a messiah that will come to earth and save His own shall become galvanized within their religious groups and organizations. These people will be considered as radical zealots or true believers. Preparation for the coming Messiah will be their primary focus in life and shall dictate their lifestyle choices.

The messianic believers will reject the world's unity religion and view it as an abomination before God. However, many sects and denominations of the messianic Churches will join with the world Church under the guides of "peace and safety". This will ultimately lead to the world Church denouncing the messianic believers and ultimately declaring them to be "enemies of the state". As a result, messianic believers will be compelled to rediscover the common roots of their faiths as Christians anticipate the return of Jesus Christ, Jews anticipate the Messiah's first coming in accordance with the prophets of the Old Testament Bible and Muslims anticipate the coming of a messiah as referenced in the Koran.

<u>Descendants of Abraham</u>

Messianic beliefs go hand in hand with monotheism (belief in one God). The most notable of the messianic faiths are Judaism, Islam and Christianity, which all stem from the seed of Abraham. The belief that God walked and communed with Abraham and established a covenant between them is shared by all (3) major monotheistic religions. Abraham was initially the father of (2) sons, Ishmael through his maidservant Hagar, and Isaac through his wife Sarah. The prophet Mohamed began the Muslim religion and was a descendent of Ishmael. Jacob (who became Israel) was the father of (12) sons that started the tribes of Israel, also known as Jews. Jesus was born of a virgin named Mary, who was a descendent of Isaac, then Israel. Therefore, these (3) Messianic faith religions shares common roots as they are all descendants of Abraham by lineage through:

- Isaac, then Jacob (Jews)
- Ishmael, then the prophet Mohammed (Muslims)
- Isaac, then Israel, then Jesus (Christians by faith)

The One True Messiah (Jesus Christ) will reveal Himself to all that diligently seek Him in anticipation of His soon return.

CHAPTER XIII

GLOBALIZATION "THE FINAL STAGE"

ECONOMIC GLOBALIZATION

World War I demonstrated to the world that war was becoming increasingly destructive and inhumane. The introduction of biological and chemical weapons coupled with the airplane being used as a war machine that could rain terror from the sky was seen as an inevitable road to the annihilation of civilization. World War I introduced the first true weapons of mass destruction that could threaten to wipe-out large populations at once.

World War II displayed how the depraved agenda of one leader over a strong sovereign nation could threaten world peace and freedom. It was determined that economic self-sufficiency along with cultural and social containment is the fuel of war. After WWI ended, the world's leading politicians began creating plans for breaking down the borders of national sovereignty and creating interdependence among the nations of the world to decrease the chance of war in the future since the reversal of technology is not an option.

After WWII world leaders crafted the framework for a system of international commerce and finance within an agreement called the Bretton Woods conference. This agreement also led to the start of international institutions that would craft and implement policies leading toward globalization.

- International Bank for Reconstruction and Development (The World Bank)
- International Monetary Fund (IMF)
- World Trade Organization (WTO)
- General Agreements on Tariffs and Trade (GATT)

MOVEMENT TOWARD GLOBALIZATION IN THE U.S.

These international organizations have made considerable progress since their inception. From the 1930's to the 1970's, most of the apparent progress was taking place in Europe primarily due to the need for reconstruction in the aftermath of World War II. To the contrary, the U.S. was seen as the leader of the free world and its people valued the sovereignty of the U.S. Therefore, in order for the U.S. to participate in the process of globalization, it would need to be dismantled and rebuilt under the auspices of globalization, being the only solution for a viable future. The late 1970's gave birth to technologies that would make it possible for the U.S. to be led ultimately into economic ruin by encouraging the exploitation of human nature through media and easy access to credit.

ECONOMIC BREAKDOWN AND WEALTH EXCHANGE MILESTONES

- Mid 1980s – Tax Code Reform
- Early 1990's – Savings and Loans Bailout
- Early 1990's – Gulf War against Iraq
- Late 1990's – dot.com Bubble Collapse
- Mid 1990's – NAFTA takes effect
- Mid 1990's – Tariffs reduced from Uruguay Round of GATT
- Late 1990's – Congress approves large tax cuts
- Early 2000's – September 11th Attacks
- Early 2000's – Invasion of Iraq
- Early 2000's – Enron files Bankruptcy
- Early 2000's – Many Major airlines file bankruptcy
- Mid 2000's – Housing Bubble Collapse
- Late 2000's – Wall Street Bailout (TARP)
- Late 2000's – General Motors files Bankruptcy

- Late 2000's – Lehman Brothers becomes insolvent
- Late 2000's – Wall Street Bailout
- Late 2000's – AIG Bailout

Each milestone represents the continuous breakdown of the U.S. economy and the exchange of wealth. In 2008, the U.S. elected Barack Obama as president. He was known to be culturally liberal and a supporter of globalization. His first initiative was the Recovery Act in response to the economic devastation that had taken place resulting from the collapse of the U.S. housing market. The sovereignty and security of the American people had finally been breached through the loss of home equity, loss of investments for retirement and loss of industry all at once for the country's largest generation.

BI-PARTISAN CONTRIBUTION TO EROSION OF AMERICA'S FOUNDATION

PRESIDENTS	TERMS	Dem	Rep	Critical Breakdown
Carter	1976-1980	4 Yrs.		Undermine Judeo-Christian Moral Standards
Reagan	1981-1988		8 Yrs.	National Debt
G.H. Bush	1989-1992		4 Yrs.	National Sovereignty / Education
Clinton	1993-2000	8 Yrs.		Undermine Judeo-Christian Moral Standards / Wealth Transfer
G.W. Bush	2001-2008		8 Yrs.	Privacy / Wealth Transfer / Education
Obama	2009-2016	8 Yrs.		Undermine Judeo-Christian Moral Standards / National Debt
TOTAL YEARS IN POWER		**20 Yrs.**	**20 Yrs.**	**40 Year Decline**

CULTURAL GLOBALIZATION

The modern world has become connected through electronic communications and multi-media venues mainly facilitated through the internet. Consequently, this unprecedented connectivity has promoted and supported access and exposure between cultures of all kinds from around the globe. The world's younger generations, primarily those born after 1970, are ever becoming culturally bound together through shared sentiments regarding government oppression and the desire for access to electronic media. This cultural globalization movement shall be the catalyst that brings down sovereign governments and forges the united global community government.

THE UNITED GLOBAL COMMUNITY (UGC)

World organizations that will pave the way to global unity and lead the masses shall include:

- United Nations (UN)
- North Atlantic Treaty Organization (NATO)
- European Union (EU)

Our present-day society is faced with many challenges that are unprecedented and unparalleled throughout the history of the world. Technology has redefined the boundaries of society from being regional, national or even continental to that of global. The internet, and the basic premise that it represents, is the most effective and efficient means of communication imaginable (at this time). This technology is here to stay.

As society in the "real world" continually becomes a place of agony and hardship, the vast and growing "virtual world" offered through the internet and multi-dimensional media becomes an "optional reality" of choice for many. The internet is rapidly becoming the world's primary means of communication, entertainment, social interaction and business transactions.

It is inevitable that the United States of America will assimilate into the greater United Global Community (UGC) likely to be led by the European Union along with other powerful regimes from the Far East. Governments will make use of the common infrastructure facilitated by the internet to quickly bring themselves into alignment with each other.

As men look to themselves for a solution to the world's problems, they will conclude that anything is possible if they are united. The mind of man without the mind of God has no choice but to reach this conclusion. Unification of mankind is not a new concept. God has acknowledged the capabilities of a united mankind when the Tower of Babel was being constructed. As always, man will seek to exalt his position over the One who created him, which will ultimately lead to his downfall.

[Genesis 11:6]

THE FIRST CENTURY CHURCH MOVEMENT (FCCM)

Once again, God's people are being faced with the threat of persecution from civil society as the Christians of the Roman Empire did in the early Church. Persecution is brought about when governments feel the need to require total allegiance of all its citizens for the sake of the republic. As a result of the extreme challenges being encountered by all nations on earth, total allegiance to a unified government will be required.

I believe that Christians in America will unite to form a community with a culture that returns to its roots found in the First Century Church Movement (FCCM). Church leaders from around the world will be led and connected through the commonality of Christian culture and the Holy Spirit. The FCCM culture shall be supported by an organized system of Commerce and Financial Services that is electronically connected through the internet, intranet systems, and other means.

The electronic infrastructure of the FCCM shall interface with the First Century Church Community at a systemic level. However, distribution to members of the FCCM shall be exclusively rendered through FCCM Lifestyle Centers and strategic industrial, commercial and retail partners along with service providers. The Church must remain accessible to everyone in the world. We must not isolate ourselves from the world if we are to be Salt and Light.

[Matthew 5:13-16]

The FCCM will remain in operation until the Holy Spirit leaves the world, as it will be sustained "directly" by the power of God. I believe that Christians in America are "circumstantially" the best candidates for supporting and promoting this endeavor due to the "necessity" caused by the recession of 2008. The nation responsible for sending the world into economic despair giving rise to Church unification and a global Christian system of exchange is reminiscent of God's will displayed through such irony that has been seen time and time again throughout history.

[22:19-21 NIV]

I believe that Christians in America will play a supporting role in this endeavor for such a time as this, being that there is no mention (in the bible) of this country's influence as a nation in the last days approaching the return of Christ. As the sovereignty of this mighty nation is challenged, the sovereignty of the Church shall be revived.

[page left blank]

CHAPTER XIV

THE MODERN ERA OF CHURCH ACCOUNTABILITY

UNITED STOREHOUSE INTERNATIONAL

Striving toward God's best while preparing for perilous times

ESTABLISHING A MINDSET TOWARD THE FUTURE

In order for the U.S. to survive the global geopolitical and economic paradigm changes of our generation, American families must adjust their standards of living. As a nation, we must adopt a sustainable "base" standard of living that will support the average working class citizen. *Christians* should focus on becoming people with extraordinary personal discipline. I believe that we must be **Resourceful** like the *Amish* community, **Conservative** like the *Scandinavians* and **Efficient** like the *Japanese* in order to build strength and viability for future generations.

Government alone will not succeed in its attempts to lead the American people into recovery. Partisanship in government inherently leads to division by design. Unity is required for success and survival in the days ahead. Many Americans are becoming unemployed and incapable of sustaining their lifestyle. Government assistance to these individuals and families does not begin to address the critical needs of average families living the "so-called" American dream before losing their job. What makes matters worse is the fact that there is no alternative sustainable lifestyle that exists in America today that is easily accessible to the average citizen.

Private industry has been focused on profits and increasing the wealth of its investors while government has been sidetracked by politics, partisanship, and special interest. A joint public-private sector initiative must emerge and provide a sustainable lifestyle alternative to what was known as the "American Dream" which has simply become a pathway to debt and dissatisfaction for most. Such an initiative must encompass the basic pillars of life in civil society without loss of civil rights and liberties.

Essentially, we must return to many of the founding principles that this great nation was built upon. We must promote Life, Liberty and the **"Pursuit of Sustainability"** along with **"Personal Responsibility"**. The pursuit of happiness is a personal ambition that has been exploited and abused and should not be "unduly" promoted. Many have invoked their constitutional right to the pursuit of happiness at the "disproportionate" expense of the general public as evidenced by what has taken place in the financial sector leading to the 2008 recession.

CHRISTIAN ECONOMIC CYCLE

As Christians, our perspective toward economics and prosperity should be biblically-based and rooted in sound doctrine. These principles date back to the days of Abraham when the concept of tithing was first introduced. These principles were further set by the Apostle Peter and those who took part in the establishment of the first Church.

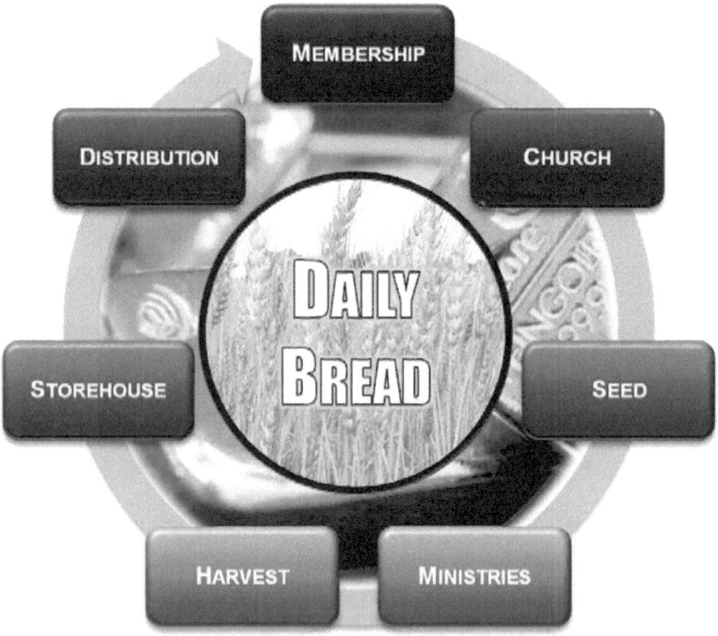

There are (7) basic components to the Christian Economic Cycle:

1. People are to give tithes and offerings to the local Church.
2. Churches are to be wise and faithful stewards of its resources.
3. Churches sew into various initiatives that the congregation supports.

4. Carry out the missions of the Church according to its mandates.
5. The results are measured through seeds planted and ministry functions.
6. Management and accounting of resources are controlled by appointed Church leaders.
7. The needs of the congregation are met through the Church.

NO DISTINCTION BY WEALTH PRINCIPLE

As humans, we all have a natural desire for relationships built upon mutual respect and a "sense" of equality. Men, in particular, should always be made to feel like valued contributors in their surroundings if they are expected to connect in a meaningful way. Similar to what is experienced at a social gathering where games are being played, in order to increase the number of players, you must adjust the rules and conditions (if necessary) to even the playing field for all participants. It is imperative that the members of the Church are always made to feel they are an important and "well-regarded" part of the body of Christ.

Having no distinction by wealth as a fundamental principle allow for all members of a community to live together in a culture that does not promote or reward elitism or materialism shown through outward displays of wealth by those who have more financial resources than others. I believe that the first century Church found this to be true and practiced this principle. Jesus warned us about the folly of serving and giving to be seen or acknowledged by others. By doing so, we forfeit our Heavenly rewards in the process. Jesus goes as far as to say that we should give in secrecy as God the Father is aware and shall reward us accordingly.

[Matthew 6:1-4]

THE BELIEVERS SHARE THEIR POSSESSIONS

In order for Christians of the early Church to survive economically, they had to participate in the free-market system of their day in some capacity. This would have produced income on an ongoing basis that would have inevitably restored wealth to the gifted, talented and hard-working, much like today's society. The system was greatly supported by those with wealth so that it could absorb the expenses of those in need. Consequently, their "common culture" made it possible for them to serve God as one body and ensure that there was no one among them in need.

[Acts 4:34-35]

Though it is reported in the book of Acts that Church members sold all they had and shared all things in common, their re-accumulation of wealth is not mentioned. There is no historical information that seems to indicate that the early Church practiced "communism" or "socialism" as many have "mistakenly" believed. To the contrary, most of the early Church was located in provinces under rule by the Roman Empire. Rome was a free-market society much like western civilization is today.

RESOURCE MANAGEMENT DEACONS

I believe that Church leadership should take inventory of gifts, talents and capabilities of each member for the sake of resource management. Church Deacons should be in charge of this process and have access to a Church resource data base. These Deacons should have a specific designation, such as "Resource Management Deacon" (RMD), not to be confused with any other type of Deacon that may be within a Church's leadership structure. RMD's should meet the biblical standards of Church leadership. They should be known to the Church leadership as being "full of the Spirit and wisdom" as Peter stipulated in the process of choosing the first RMD's as found in Acts 6:1-7.

The Church congregation should be equally divided into seven groups. Each group will be assigned to an RMD that shall be responsible for ensuring that the needs of the people are being addressed. RMD's (and their staff if needed) shall keep track of each member's current status and be aware of extraordinary circumstances that may exist in their lives. The RMD's should always be informed about who among them is in need and who among them has plenty. RMD's shall also be responsible for finding ways to encourage regular fellowship between members outside of the Church setting. A Resource Management Deacon should be like the ultimate "Christian" life coach or lifestyle manager.

RESOURCE MANAGEMENT DEPARTMENT – BASIC HIERARCHY

(Church / USI Interface)

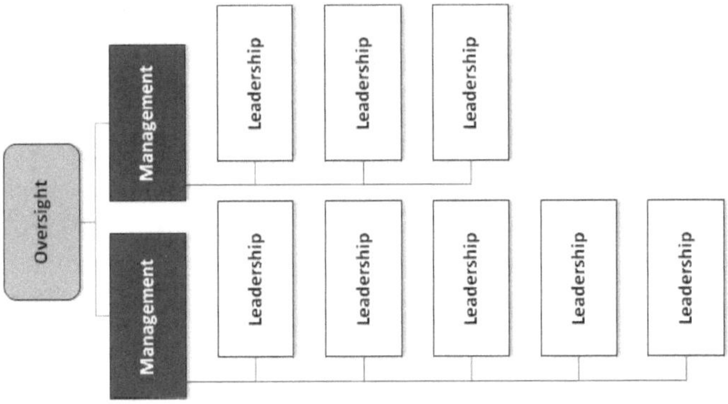

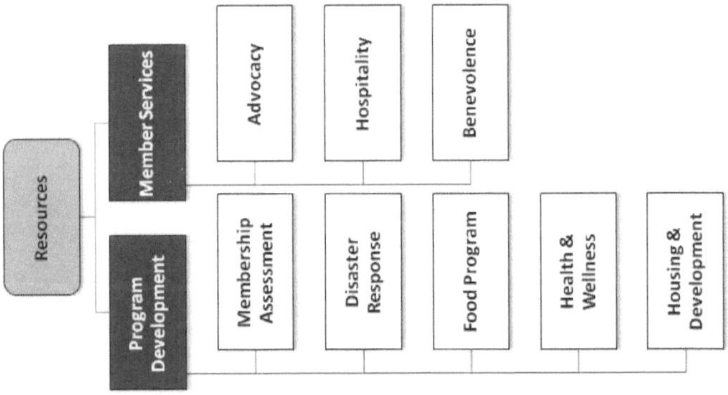

UNDERWRITERS / ASSETS MANAGEMENT

There will be some among the Church membership having "significant" or relatively "vast" wealth. They should be given the opportunity to become Underwriters for the Church. Understanding and acknowledging that God is the source of all wealth and the concept of stewardship allows those who are blessed with extraordinary financial resources to be used for God's will in the building of His kingdom.

These individuals would be contacted by an executive level Pastor, or designee, requesting them to review proposals that have been deemed as "worthy projects" by Church executive leadership but lacking adequate funding. These individuals would be looked to as a source of "wise counsel" and potentially "financial support".

As an example, projects may range from meeting the needs of an individual or family in the Church that has been devastated by a natural disaster or loss of income to a building project for the expansion of a ministry. Financial backing may range from cash donations to collateralization for Church development endeavors. Jesus pointed out the "extreme difficulty" for those with great wealth to give it away to the poor and follow Him as He has instructed. Therefore, it is anticipated that only those who are truly led by the Spirit of God and called for this purpose will be able to meet this challenge.

[Matthew 19:21-26]

THE ENDEAVOR

United Storehouse International (USI) is proposed to be an organization established by a group comprised of Church Leaders and Christian Businessmen from around the country and ultimately around the world. USI seeks to present the opportunity for Churches of every denomination to "equitably" partake in a program that provides tangible benefits to the members of its congregations, families in their local communities and other households in need.

This endeavor is an unprecedented mission to establish a membership based benefits cooperative with a potential for infinite growth. Though reminiscent of a discount club or government entitlement program, there are distinct differences between USI's lifestyle program and other such programs, including, but not limited to:

- USI is proposed to be a private non-profit organization, not a for-profit venture or government agency
- USI offers benefits to its members, not dividends or entitlements
- USI shall operate and provide benefits based on its assets rather than speculation or debt

There are also, notable similarities, such as:

- USI is ultimately a system that is overseen and controlled by representatives elected by the people being served
- USI offers benefits that provide critical supplements to the lives of its members

USI provides a sense of security to members of the Church that are in "good standing" in a time of crisis or transition through providing access to a broad variety of "essential" goods, services and benefits, including, but not limited to:

- Crisis Intervention

- Access to USI Food Banks and Retail Outlets
- Emergency Household Assistance
- Emergency Shelter & Transitional Housing

USI PROJECT 4-MAJOR FUNCTIONS

PROMOTION OF SUSTAINABLE CONSERVATIVE CHRISTIAN LIFESTYLES

The integrity of the mission, which is to promote and support a sustainable Christian lifestyle, is the "meat" of the program. The USI lifestyle is proposed as an essential supplement to the fast-paced western civilization and capitalist economy. The main objective is to bring recognition and establishment of a common Christian lifestyle that is supported in a practical and tangible way by the Church.

The USI lifestyle offers an alternative to secularism without using isolation or segregation from mainstream society as a fundamental premise. USI seeks to be a positive influence to the societal establishment as it helps its members to appreciate and adopt a conservative and sustainable Christian lifestyle in an ever growing secular culture.

CHRISTIAN LIFESTYLE CENTERS AND COMMUNITY DEVELOPMENT

The USI lifestyle program is designed to operate on the "skeleton" of its strategic partnerships and distribution points. USI will initially seek to place its Lifestyle Centers and Communities in densely populated Urban and Suburban communities. A variation of the USI Lifestyle Centers will be offered to select rural communities as well. Existing retail units will also be evaluated and considered for redevelopment. Making sure that all USI development projects "fully" meet the criteria established is critical for long term success. The development of USI Lifestyle Centers and Communities shall present potential opportunities for select investment partners to participate through providing short-term financing or bridge loans.

MANAGEMENT OF BENEFIT DISTRIBUTION TO MEMBERS

The benefits being managed and distributed to its members is the *"life-blood"* of the program. This process shall be primarily executed by use of bar coding on the same platform as normal credit cards in alignment with industry standard. Members shall be issued cards and USI distribution points shall be equipped with card readers as found in most retail outlets throughout the world. The members shall be able to use these cards for USI transactions on the internet as well. As the USI program network grows, adding new strategic partners and alliances along with access to additional benefits shall increase accordingly.

USI shall facilitate the administration, management and operation of the benefits distribution system. Managing the benefits distribution shall be financially supported by a portion of the program fees received from its partners and sponsors along with transaction fees from participating strategic alliances that provide discounts or benefits to USI members.

ADMINISTRATION AND FUNDRAISING

In essence, USI shall facilitate and operate a benefits management company, (that operates similarly to a credit card company), overseen by a Board of Directors comprised of representatives elected by USI members with proceeds being reinvested into the USI program as its prime directive.

The opportunity to partake in the establishment of USI is a privilege extended to select individuals, entities and organizations having displayed their willingness to be accountable and faithful stewards of God's wealth and feel led to become an investment partner. USI shall seek to partner with such individuals, entities and organizations that have been financially blessed who recognize and accept their role as a supporter of this project.

SUPPORT AND DISTRIBUTION CYCLE

This diagram illustrates the core cycle of the USI program.

1. USI members support their local Church
2. The Church becomes a USI partner
3. USI facilitates development projects and programs for the Church
4. USI programs provide essential goods and services to members

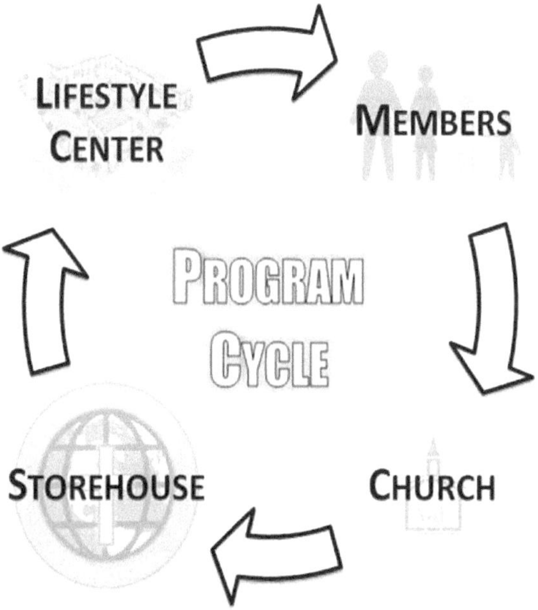

TYPICAL "SUBURBAN" LIFESTYLE CENTER - CONCEPTUAL DESIGN

This rendering depicts a typical "plaza-style" Lifestyle Center. Each USI Center shall include resource outlets such as:

1. Cafeteria Style Restaurant
    - Bakery & Coffee Shop
2. General Store
    - Household Goods & Produce Stand
3. Thrift and Consignment
    - Clothing Alterations & Repair
4. Women's Health & Beauty
5. Barber Shop
6. Indoor Fun & Games
7. Community Resource Center

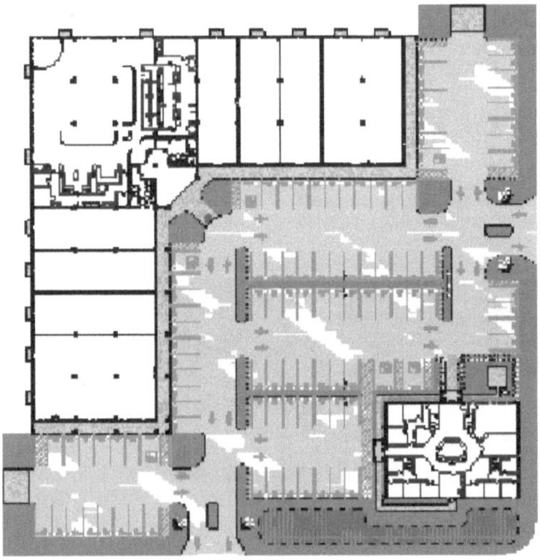

PROGRAM STRUCTURE AND PARTNERSHIPS

Lifestyle Centers shall be owned and operated by a local Church sponsor. Approved Church Cooperatives and Anchor Churches shall be eligible to be considered for sponsorship according to a membership criteria similar to the following examples.

(Based on average family = 4 people)

Satellite Churches are congregations with less than 50 families. Satellites must be affiliated with a Coop or Anchor Church to be eligible for membership to USI.

Community Churches are congregations with more than 50 families and less than 150. Community Churches must be affiliated with a Coop or Anchor Church to be eligible for membership to USI.

Church Cooperatives are a group of Churches forming an alliance having more than 450 families. A USI approved Coop may offer USI membership to its congregations. USI Coops may be eligible for Lifestyle Center Sponsorship.

Anchor Churches are congregations with more than 450 families. A USI approved Anchor Church may offer SI membership to its congregations. Anchor Churches are eligible for Lifestyle Center Sponsorship.

MEMBERSHIP DUES

The original USI model is being designed with the goal of being able to operate on a budget derived from 2% of an average tithe. Tithing standards shall be derived from US Census information regarding the Average Median Income (AMI) in different regions of the United States. Based on the latest Census Tract information and factoring in the current economic conditions, a national AMI of $45,000.00 per year is being used for strategic planning purposes.

MEMBER

AMI		→	$	45,000.00 *Annual salary*
Tithes	52 *weeks*	=	$	86.54 *weekly*

CHURCH

Tithers	*x* 450	→	$	38,942.31 *weekly*

STOREHOUSE

Fees	2%	→	$	778.85 *weekly*

THE PROJECTED INITIAL COST OF MEMBERSHIP PER HOUSEHOLD WOULD BE

$1.73 PER WEEK

NOTE: THIS IS AN EXAMPLE OF AN ESTIMATE BASED ON MINIMUM OPERATIONAL EXPENSES UNDER 2010 ECONOMIC CONDITIONS THAT ARE SUBJECT TO CONSTANT AND DRAMATIC CHANGE IN ACCORDANCE WITH CHANGES IN THE ECONOMY.

GENERAL PROGRAM SERVICES – DEPARTMENTAL OUTLINE

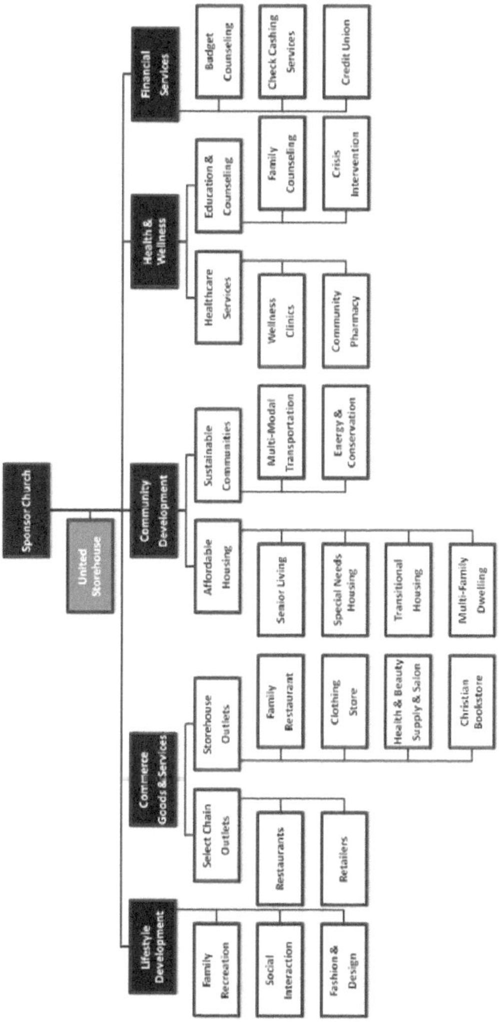

BASIC PHILOSOPHY

USI seeks to establish precedence that changes the paradigm for Christian living in today's modern society. As Christians, we believe that it is our duty to facilitate opportunities for our families to live and thrive in the world but not be consumed by it. Jesus refers to us as the Light of the World.

[Matthew 2:14 NIV]

THE MISSION

USI is focused on supporting the Body of Christ while the Church is focused of being light and salt to the world.

PRIMARY GOALS:

1. To support the "figurative" rebuilding of the Church walls by addressing "common needs" within the Church community at-large.
2. To assist "individual Church bodies" with creating points of interaction toward establishing a unified culture within that is postured for compatibility with the greater Church community at-large.
3. To promote a conservative and sustainable lifestyle by establishing a worldwide network that provides access to essential goods and services to families at a local community level.
4. To provide additional benefits for members by gaining access to significant cost reductions for essential goods and services through local USI centers and providers worldwide.
5. To create a venue by which members of all financial and social backgrounds have access to the same high-quality goods and services without differential. (Availability of

goods and services may vary based on seasonal and regional demographics)

6. To encourage the general public to visit their local Church and consider joining as a result of their seeking access to USI membership, thereby exposing them to the Gospel of Jesus Christ and furthering the mission of the gospel.
7. To become an advocate and economic support mechanism for the Church and other Christian organizations serving the cause of Christ throughout the world.

KEY OBJECTIVES:

1. Church Administrative Infrastructure Support
    - To revisit the original management protocol and design of the Church and the role of Deacons.
    - To support restoration of Church infrastructure to a level of integrity that resembles the first century Church but modified to operate in today's modern society.
    - To support restoration of the Deacon's role as "Primary advocates" in matters pertaining to the overall "well-being" of Church members and church business.
    - To support restoration of the Deacon's role as Resource Managers toward serving and meeting the needs of the Church and its members.
2. Church Cohesion
    - To establish points of connection between all Church groups through promoting the establishment of a "Biblically-based" and "mutually accepted" Christian cultural standards.

- To promote "systematic interactions and transactions" between Church groups on a local, regional and international levels.

3. Christian Resource Management

- To illuminate facts about the world's perspective toward economics in contrast to a "biblically-based" Christian perspective and propose viable alternatives.
- To provide a means of stabilizing household finances through participating in a Christian economic system network accessed through the local Church.
- To provide oversight, management and distribution of benefits to Members and equity to Investors, Strategic Partners and Service Providers.
- To provide guidance, technical support and assistance to Members, Investors, Strategic Partners and Service Providers.
- To continuously seek opportunities for program enhancements and expansion.

CREDIBILITY BY: ACCOUNTABILITY, FAITHFULNESS AND STEWARDSHIP (AFAS)

In America, a person's character and financial viability is determined by a credit score. USI seeks to determine such viability through accountability. Many privileges will be offered that will require a certain level of integrity displayed by the member being served. Accountability, faithfulness and stewardship exhibited and observed in their local Church are the key factors being considered. However, if a member is not able to obtain credit through conventional lending institutions and is in need of credit being extended for goods or

services rendered through USI, the designated USI official of the member's local Church can authorize credit from the Church's USI credit line until accountability is established for future personal credit with USI member services. Each USI certified Church partner will receive a line of credit from USI to be used as collateral for members in need along with rechargeable USI gift cards for non-members in need that the Church wishes to extend USI goods and services to instead of cash.

COMMUNITY THROUGH COOPERATIVES

Many Americans have become convinced that a person's self-worth is connected to their material possessions. Many Christians subconsciously believe that to die with the most things somehow indicates a life of success even though the teachings of Jesus repeatedly warn us against storing up our treasures on earth and the negative consequences associated with this practice.

[Matthew 6:19-20]

USI seeks to provide an organized venue by which members can assign (lend with conditions) or donate seldom used items in good working condition. Participating members would have access to all kinds of items, primarily made available by members, being cataloged and kept in a warehouse to be loaned out for members use. The benefits include a tax write-off for donated items, low-cost access to items that would be impractical to own, and clearing out space in garages, sheds, storage facilities, etc... In like fashion, USI seeks to recycle clothing and other goods that members consign or donate. This system also promotes the option of household mobility in a more "transient" society.

SETTING PRECEDENCE

All USI endeavors shall be administered, managed, operated and executed according to the highest standards of professionalism and accountability that is "feasibly" possible. As a private non-profit organization, USI shall seek to set new standards and trends among its peers by remaining focused on the mission of promoting a conservative Christian lifestyle. Much of the surplus funds gained by USI shall be reinvested for the expansion of services and benefits to partners and members instead of focusing on expanding executive compensation. USI shall stand out as a unique organization in a capitalistic western society.

ESTABLISHING COALITIONS

THE OBJECTIVE

The main objective toward establishing coalitions is to promote, Connectivity, Congruency, Consistency, Continuity, and Compatibility between all Christian organizations and Church groups.

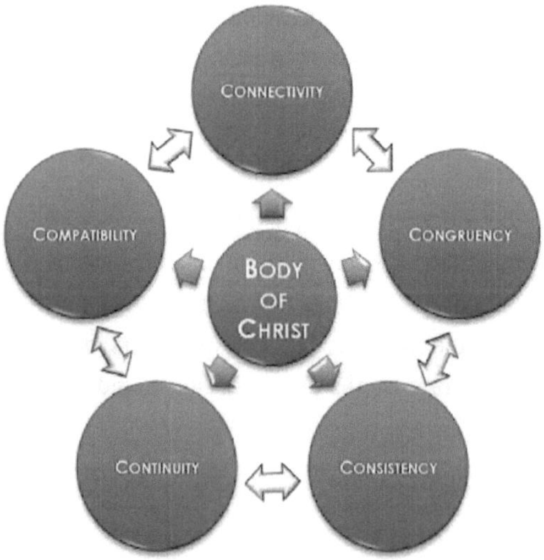

LOCAL PARTNERS

The USI program is designed to succeed as a "stand alone" initiative at the local Church level as well as a "broad-based" network program on an international scale. Considerable emphasis will be placed on building coalitions with local Church groups promoting self-contained full operational usage of the USI program within each sovereign Church organization. The goal is that each Church operates in a manner that is compatible with other Church groups that are part of the USI network.

GLOBAL PARTNERS

USI shall seek to form coalitions with other like-minded, mainstream Christian organizations known for providing support operations including, but not limited to groups like: Samaritan's Purse, Moody Bible Institute, Metropolitan Ministries, Feed the Children and many others.

USI shall seek to partner with Church organizations that may already be operating similar programs that were designed to meet the needs of a smaller demographic while encouraging the formation of new organizations that seek to be a part of USI's vision for promoting interconnection between Churches and international reciprocation of membership benefits. We want to support and use the best ideas being practiced within the Church and make them available to all Christian organizations that desire to participate.

[Proverbs 11:14]

U.S. REGION ADMINISTRATIVE STRUCTURE

The organization shall be led by a regional president appointed by a regional board of directors. The regional president will appoint a board Chair from among the elected regional board members.

The U.S. region should be divided into seven distinct sections. Each section should consist of states that are geographically contiguous, with the exception of Alaska, Hawaii, U.S. territories and the Caribbean Islands. Each section will have a strategically placed headquarters that will house regional corporate functions for United Storehouse International.

Each section should have a board of directors comprised of seven Church leaders elected by delegates representing the USI partners throughout the section. A sectional president shall be elected by the board. The sectional president will appoint a board Chair from among the elected sectional board members.

Each section will break down into Areas and Districts. The hierarchy of administration and election processes shall repeat accordingly at each level.

INTERNATIONAL REGION-1 (USA) SECTIONAL DEMARCATION – EXAMPLE

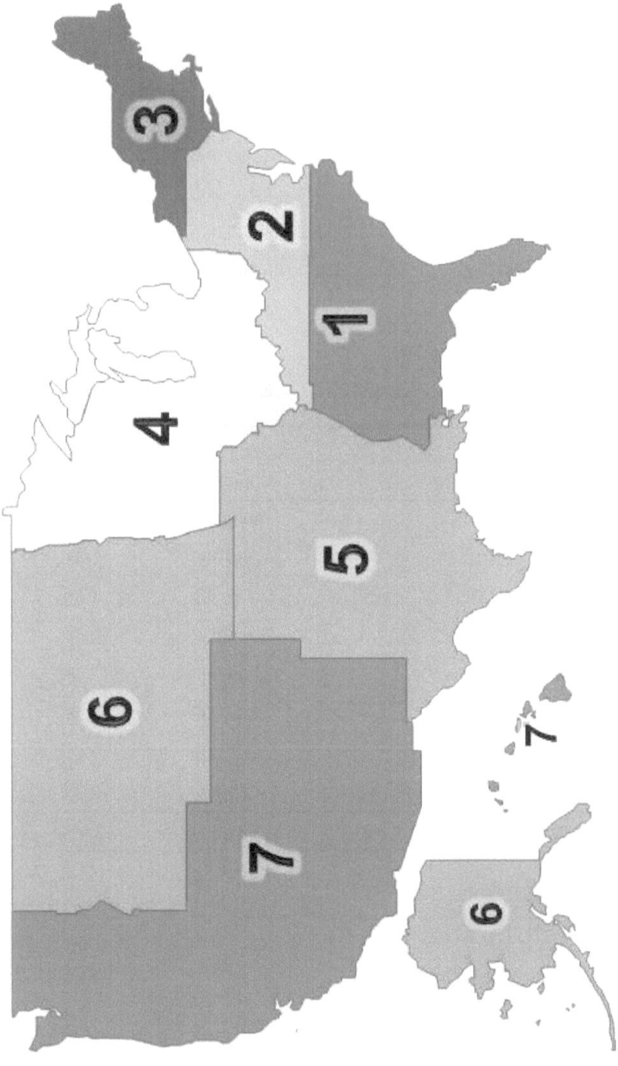

Example of States within U.S. Storehouse Sections

2009 U.S. Census Data rounded to nearest 100k

SECTION - 1			Population	Pct.	
1	AL	ALABAMA	4,700,000	1.5%	
2	FL	FLORIDA	18,500,000	6.0%	✝ Tampa Bay
3	GA	GEORGIA	9,800,000	3.2%	
4	MS	MISSISSIPPI	3,000,000	1.0%	
5	NC	NORTH CAROLINA	9,400,000	3.0%	
6	SC	SOUTH CAROLINA	4,600,000	1.5%	
7	TN	TENNESSEE	6,300,000	2.0%	
	PR	PUERTO RICO	4,000,000	1.3%	
	VI	US VIRGIN ISLANDS	100,000	0.0%	
TOTAL SECTIONAL POPULATION			**60,400,000**	**19.4%**	

SECTION - 2			Population	Pct.	
1	DE	DELAWARE	900,000	0.3%	
2	KY	KENTUCKY	4,300,000	1.4%	
3	MD	MARYLAND	5,700,000	1.8%	
4	NJ	NEW JERSEY	8,700,000	2.8%	
5	PA	PENNSYLVANIA	12,600,000	4.1%	✝ Pittsburg
6	VA	VIRGINIA	7,900,000	2.5%	
7	WV	WEST VIRGINIA	1,800,000	0.6%	
	DC	DISTRICT OF COLUMBIA	600,000	0.2%	
TOTAL SECTIONAL POPULATION			**42,500,000**	**13.7%**	

SECTION - 3	Population	Pct.	
1 CT CONNECTICUT	3,500,000	1.1%	
2 ME MAINE	1,300,000	0.4%	
3 MA MASSACHUSETTS	6,600,000	2.1%	
4 NH NEW HAMPSHIRE	1,300,000	0.4%	
5 NY NEW YORK	19,500,000	6.3%	✝ New York
6 RI RHODE ISLAND	1,100,000	0.4%	
7 VT VERMONT	600,000	0.2%	
TOTAL SECTIONAL POPULATION	**33,900,000**	**10.9%**	

SECTION - 4	Population	Pct.	
1 MI MICHIGAN	10,000,000	3.2%	
2 IN INDIANA	6,400,000	2.1%	
3 IL ILLINOIS	12,900,000	4.2%	✝ Chicago
4 IA IOWA	3,000,000	1.0%	
5 MN MINNESOTA	5,300,000	1.7%	
6 OH OHIO	11,500,000	3.7%	
7 WI WISCONSIN	5,700,000	1.8%	
TOTAL SECTIONAL POPULATION	**54,800,000**	**17.6%**	

SECTION - 5	Population	Pct.	
1 AR ARKANSAS	2,900,000	0.9%	
2 KS KANSAS	2,800,000	0.9%	
3 LA LOUISIANA	4,500,000	1.4%	
4 MO MISSOURI	6,000,000	1.9%	
5 OK OKLAHOMA	3,700,000	1.2%	
6 TX TEXAS	24,800,000	8.0%	✝ Dallas
TOTAL SECTIONAL POPULATION	**44,700,000**	**14.4%**	

SECTION - 6	Population	Pct.	
1 AK ALASKA	700,000	0.2%	
2 CO COLORADO	5,000,000	1.6%	✝ Col. Springs
3 ID IDAHO	1,500,000	0.5%	
4 MT MONTANA	1,000,000	0.3%	
5 NE NEBRASKA	1,800,000	0.6%	
6 ND NORTH DAKOTA	650,000	0.2%	
7 SD SOUTH DAKOTA	800,000	0.3%	
8 UT UTAH (Mormons)	***2,800,000***	***0.9%***	***Salt Lake City***
9 WY WYOMING	500,000	0.2%	
TOTAL SECTIONAL POPULATION	**14,050,000**	**4.5%**	

SECTION - 7	Population	Pct.	
1 AZ ARIZONA	6,600,000	2.1%	
2 CA CALIFORNIA	36,961,664	11.9%	✝ Los Angeles
3 HI HAWAII	1,300,000	0.4%	
4 NV NEVADA	2,600,000	0.8%	
5 NM NEW MEXICO	2,000,000	0.6%	
6 OR OREGON	3,800,000	1.2%	
7 WA WASHINGTON	6,700,000	2.2%	
GUAM	200,000	0.1%	
NORTHERN MARIANAS	100,000	0.0%	
AMERICAN SAMOA	100,000	0.0%	
TOTAL SECTIONAL POPULATION	**60,361,664**	**19.4%**	

2010 Est. Total Region-1 Population	**310,711,664**	**100%**

USI DISTRIBUTION NETWORK

Each section will be assessed to determine what its greatest assets and needs are and what they are projected to be in the future. This assessment will include, but not be limited to:

- Geography
- Natural resources
- Climate
- Industry
- Transportation Infrastructure
- Socio-Political Dynamics

Based on the results of the assessment, inter-sectional trade and exchange cooperatives will be crafted. A nationwide commerce and distribution network system shall be established. USI lifestyle centers shall be provided with regular deliveries of supplies from points of origin around the country. A division of USI shall administrate and coordinate all orders and deliveries from distribution centers strategically located in each section, most likely placed in the same location as the section's corporate headquarters.

[page left blank]

COMPONENTS WITHIN THE MODERN CHURCH

Body Make-Up of The Modern Church (example)

PARTS & FUNCTIONS WITHIN THE BODY

AGE GROUPS

A. **INFANTS**
   0 -23 MOS.

B. **TODDLERS**
   2 -4 YEARS

C. **CHILDREN**
   5-11 YEARS

D. **YOUTH**
   12-17 YEARS

E. **YOUNG ADULTS**
   18-34 YEARS

F. **MATURE ADULTS**
   35-54 YEARS

G. **SENIORS**
   55-74 YEARS

H. **ELDERLY**
   75 YEARS +

LEVELS & POSITIONS

I. **WORKERS (LAITY)**
   - *WORKERS*
   - *HELPERS*
   - *CRAFTSMEN*

II. **SUPERVISORS (LEADERS)**
   - *TEACHERS*
   - *TRAINERS*
   - *INSTRUCTORS*

III. **MANAGERS (DEACONS)**
   - *COORDINATORS*
   - *PROGRAM MANAGERS*
   - *ADMINISTRATORS*

IV. **OVERSEERS (ELDERS)**
   - *EVALUATORS*
   - *PLANNERS*
   - *DIRECTORS*

V. **EXECUTIVES (PASTORS)**
   - *STRATEGISTS*
   - *VISIONARIES*
   - *PASTORS*

MEMBERSHIP CELLS

LEADERS
- *MEMBER ADVOCATE MANAGER*

FAMILIES
- *MATRIARCHS*
  - *CHILDREN*
    - *GRANDCHILDREN*

INDIVIDUALS

PROGRAMS

OVERSEER
- *ELDER*

MANAGER(S)
- *PROGRAM MANAGER*

SUPERVISOR(S)
- *(PER PROGRAM MANAGER)*

WORKER(S)
- *(PER PROGRAM MANAGER)*

CONSIDERATION FACTORS

AGE GROUPS
- *(PER PROGRAM OVERSEER)*

SPIRITUAL GIFTS
- *(PER PROGRAM OVERSEER)*

SPIRITUAL GIFTS

(A) WISDOM (B) KNOWLEDGE (C) FAITH (D) HEALING (E) PROPHECY (F) DISCERNMENT (G) TONGUES (H) INTERPRETATION

MODERN CHURCH DEPARTMENTAL ORGANIZATION CHART (EXAMPLE)

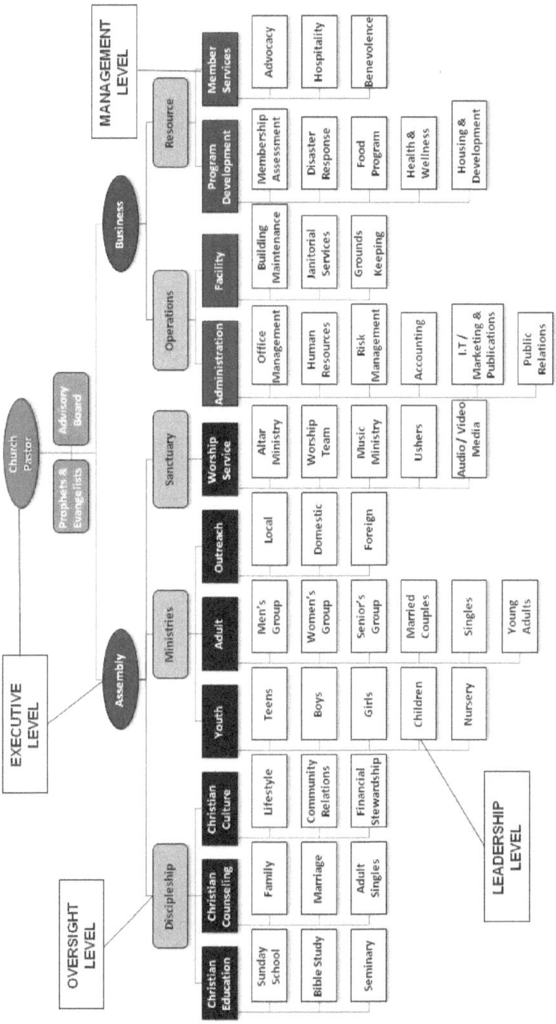

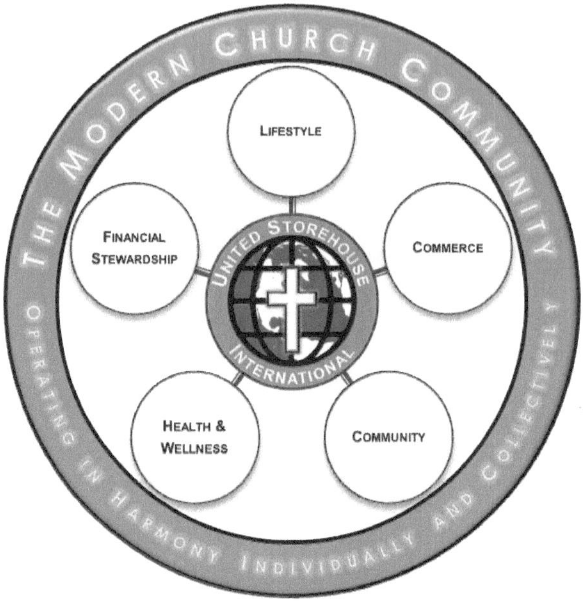

LIFESTYLE

USI seeks to influence, support and promote a lifestyle based on conservative Christian values with consideration toward the contemporary western culture that we live in. Each USI Center shall be equipped with a Lifestyle component. This component shall include, but not be limited to:

LIFESTYLE COUNSELING

USI shall support and provide guidance in all areas that pertain to a typical lifestyle, such as energy efficiency and food preparation as examples. Professionals shall be made available to provide a detailed custom plan for members that need assistance with ideas and plans toward lifestyle restructuring.

FAMILY RECREATION / ENTERTAINMENT

USI shall provide opportunities for family recreation and entertainment that would incorporate the local community's cultural heritage while promoting the fundamental lifestyle message of USI. Such venues shall include, but not be limited to:

- Game Arcade at the Recreation Center
- Movie Nights at the Recreation Center for all age groups
- Basketball and Volleyball at the Recreation Center
- Planned Off-Site Events (If not facilitated at USI Community Center)
- Bowling
- Skating

COMMUNITY RELATIONS / SOCIAL INTERACTION

USI shall provide suggestions and support to the local Church and outreach partners in forging sound relationships and venues for social networking within the communities being served. Such venues shall include, but not be limited to:

- Community Health, Job & Career-Training Events
- Small Business Networking Events
- Holiday Events" Block Party Style"

CULTURAL DEVELOPMENT / FASHION, DESIGN AND TRENDSETTING

USI seeks to establish a brand of its own that will focus on fashion, clothing and trendsetting for youth. Talented youth members of USI shall be invited to participate in the formation and growth of this venture. Themes and décor of each USI Center and USI Community shall pay tribute to the local heritage and architecture while distinctly reflecting the fundamental lifestyle message of USI.

COMMERCE

USI shall create and promote a system of commerce and distribution that will primarily take place at the local USI Lifestyle Centers. Each USI Lifestyle Center shall be a multi-function plaza designed to facilitate the distribution of essential goods and services to families within the local community. The goal is that USI members will be able to redeem benefits at any USI Center worldwide. The word says that God's people will always have in abundance even while others may not have enough.

[Proverbs 13:25]

Such benefits shall include, but not be limited to:

- Same access to discounts on essential goods and services from any USI Center worldwide
- Access to USI Community Recreation Center amenities worldwide
- Emergency assistance from any USI partner Church or organization worldwide
- USI Credit Extended

COMMUNITY DEVELOPMENT

USI shall promote and facilitate the design and development of sustainable residential communities. The USI Communities main focus shall be geared toward being a complimentary component to the USI Lifestyle in conjunction with the USI Centers. There shall be a variety of approaches to promoting USI community living.

Initial development models shall be focused on accommodating the elderly and permanently disabled with emphasis on war veterans and the developmentally disabled. These segments of our population are growing and significantly underserved. Other development models shall be designed to accommodate median and low income working families along with those in need of transitional housing due to job loss or loss of income.

ON-SITE

Members that reside in a USI Planned Development Community shall have the privilege of being in a self-contained community environment designed for living the USI Lifestyle. Among many other advantages, transportation in the form of shuttles would be available to all residents to points within the community, the USI Center and local Church partner facilities.

OFF-SITE

Members that reside in nearby communities will have the opportunity to share the benefits of a USI Community by having access to select features and amenities. USI Community Centers shall facilitate and offer a variety of recreational programs and entertainment events suitable for people of all ages and families.

HEALTH AND WELLNESS

USI seeks to promote good health as a central and key element of the USI lifestyle. A multi-faceted approach shall be taken toward accomplishing this goal. Each USI Center or Community shall be equipped with a Health and Wellness Center. This facility will be used to provide assistance to members according to the most important needs of each local community.

HEALTHCARE SERVICES

Trained and certified Healthcare workers shall be on hand to provide assistance to members in need of help including, but not limited to:

- Health Education & Wellness Clinics
- Family Counseling evaluations & referrals
- Mental Health Assistance evaluations & referrals
- Crisis Intervention

USI shall seek to have licensed healthcare professionals volunteer their time as a remote extension of their practice on an incremental and rotating schedule basis. This service is primarily geared toward members that are unable to obtain health insurance that are in need of seeing a licensed physician, counselor or practitioner. Members shall have access to these professionals for the purpose of providing routine examinations and/or evaluations along with treating basic illnesses and prescriptions. Members shall receive referrals if their needs extend beyond the scope of service available.

Qualified professionals that volunteer their time, talents and/or expertise shall obtain a "preferred business or service provider" status with USI. Individuals or businesses that receive the preferred status will enjoy the privilege of being promoted as an affiliate partner and added to the USI endorsement referral list of businesses and professionals.

FINANCIAL STEWARDSHIP

HOUSEHOLD FINANCES

USI seeks to assist its members through providing a number of financial services designed to complement the USI lifestyle. Much of the driving force behind the USI lifestyle program is giving each member the opportunity to become empowered through restructuring their lives, which often begins with the restructuring of their debt and mentality toward personal finances. Each USI Lifestyle Center shall house a Financial Services Center. USI seeks to provide access to a number of essential financial services and tools at little to no cost for its members.

BUDGET COUNSELING

USI shall seek to partner with an organization like Crown Financial Services, a well-established Christian firm that offer a wide variety of "Biblically-based" financial management tools and programs that are fundamentally sound. USI shall provide an outlet for such programs within its Financial Services Center. Financial management classes shall be available to all members. Such classes shall be a prerequisite for members seeking financial assistance. USI shall also offer many other counseling services to members seeking guidance toward being good stewards of their finances.

[Proverbs 11:14]

GIFT COUPON EXCHANGE PROGRAM

In the wake of the current worldwide economic crisis, there are growing concerns about the stability of the monetary system, especially the U.S. dollar. In light of rising cost for all essential goods and services driven by market forces, merchants within sustainable community environments are considering alternative means of exchange outside of the world market. This concept is not new, nor is it prohibited by law. The U.S. Constitution provides for the exchange of private currency between U.S. citizens. There are a number of such currencies in existence throughout the U.S. today, most notably the Berkshire with over 3,000,000 in circulation.

I don't believe that the Church should establish a currency system in the same manner as others have. Instead, I am proposing a gift coupon system for redeeming specific goods and services being offered by participating USI partners as a hedge against the world's monetary system. By establishing uniformity in what is being offered, regional and sectional rates of exchange along with relative value of goods and services can easily be established and updated as necessary in a fair and equitable manner. In other words, every USI outlet would offer comparable goods and services that are similar in value in a given category.

For example, a typical meal might consist of a 4 ounce fruit serving or garden salad, 6 ounces of meat or protein, 12 ounces of starch, 8 ounces of vegetables and a 16 ounce drink. What is specifically offered at a particular USI outlet at any given time would depend on typical "supply and demand" factors, such as; geographic location, seasonal crop, accessibility, availability and cost of products.

Through volume purchasing and volunteer labor, this example of a typical meal might cost $2.00 to prepare. The retail market value of this meal might be $8.00 plus tax. A single gift coupon might be obtained for $5.00 from a local Church partner. A typical meal would be redeemable for one gift coupon at any participating USI outlet. In this scenario, the Church selling the coupon would retain a portion of the profit as a fundraiser while donating a small portion to USI for managing the gift coupon program. The USI outlet sponsor Church would retain the remaining portion of the profit to cover its expenses and overhead as this is a non-profit venture.

Sample Gift Credit Coupon - Conceptual Design

MEMBERSHIP & BENEFITS

As an active member of your local Church, there will likely be many opportunities to serve above and beyond what is required as a "member in good standing." There may be times when your local Church wants to bless a member in exchange for services to the Church. Gift credits can be issued to a member's account. In addition to gift coupons, each USI Church partner shall be given general account credits that can be issued through other forms of tender or administered electronically to a member's individual accounts.

Example:

The Church orders 10,000 credits of varying types. The Church receives:

- 7,000 Gift Coupons
- 1,000 Benevolence Gift Certificates
- 2,000 Electronic Account Credits

The membership card will serve as a debit card for gift coupon credits in addition to its use as identification. Member credits can be used for obtaining USI goods and services beyond what is allocated through basic membership benefits. These credits can also be used to obtain gift cards that can be used by non-members.

CHECK CASHING

Participating USI outlets may provide "limited" check cashing services to members, including, but not limited to:

- Payroll Check Cashing
- Wire Transfers of Funds
- Free Money Orders
- ATM Access

CREDIT UNION

USI shall eventually seek to form a credit union that will serve the broad financial needs of all members. Basic credit union membership shall not be denied based on a derogatory credit history. A money management class is suggested for everyone seeking to join the credit union. Loan applications shall be underwritten and processed in accordance with typical banking standards. However, loans may be underwritten by the applicant's local Church if the application is denied.

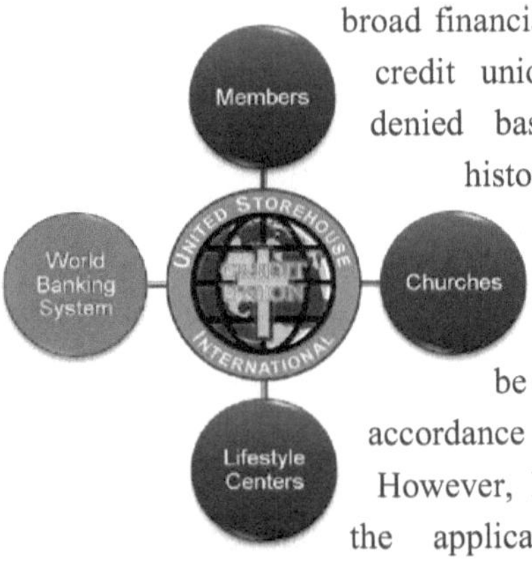

The key Credit Union services being focused on shall include, but not be limited to:

- Checking and Savings accounts available to all members
- Debit cards available to all members

- Low-Interest Personal Loans for debt restructuring (approved by USI financial counselor)
- Interest-Free Crisis Loans (approved by designated local Church official)
- Car Loans for vehicles on the USI recommended vehicles list
- Home Improvement Loans for efficiency upgrades
- Church Building Project Loans
- Investment Loans to USI approved endeavors
- Small Business Loans to qualifying members and USI Lifestyle Center vendors

MOVING THE MISSION FORWARD

ESTABLISHING A LEGACY FOR FUTURE GENERATIONS

The USI project seeks to leave a lasting legacy for generations to come. Such a movement is poised to cause results of historic proportion. The impact potential is infinite. God willing, such an endeavor may thrive up to the return of Jesus Christ as USI shall seek to be a good steward and caretaker of His bride, the Church.

[Proverbs 13:22]

As Jesus and the prophets before Him declared the return of Christ, so did they also give warning to the Church regarding the days preceding His return. Christians are subtly being forced and coerced to conform to secular lifestyle due to for-profit private business and the government's ever growing influence and control over such things as:

- Defining culture through media
- Controlling Civil rights (such as freedom of speech)
- Redefining morality / Societal norms
- Controlling Access to Commerce
- Controlling Access to Healthcare
- Controlling Use of Natural Resources

USI would be poised to act as an intermediary and advocate for the Church, strengthened by the support of its membership and partners worldwide.

[Philippians 3:13-14]

USI would stand, along with many other Christian organizations, to support and defend the rights of its members to have the opportunity for continuing to live a Christian lifestyle until the prophecy is fulfilled and our Lord and Savior, Jesus Christ, returns.

[Revelation 16:15]

ABOUT THE AUTHOR

Travis Edward Hills, Sr. has lived a life of diverse experiences that have culminated into a unique perspective toward life. His

professional experiences include being a Firefighter, a Police Officer, a business owner and a Building Contractor. His personal experiences include being married, divorced and re-married and having a blended family with a total of four-children. These "highlighted" experiences, along with many others, have allowed him to witness the harsh reality of man's fallen nature "first-hand" and endure through personal failure, eventually experiencing redemption through the blood of Jesus Christ. He believes that God has given him the privilege of serving the Church as a whole in this season. He plans to use the culmination of his life's experiences combined with his God-given gifts and talents to play a role in God's plan for the Church to become unified and positioned to be kept and blessed in these perilous times that are upon us.

[1 Corinthians 1:26-31]

Travis was born in 1969 to Thomas C. Hills, Sr. and Gwendolyn E. Hills in Compton California. The family moved to Tampa, Florida in 1972, where his parents were originally from. Travis, along with his wife Jacqueline and other family members currently reside in the Tampa Bay area as he has for most of his life. He also has 3 older siblings, Wanda, Thomas, and Tonya.

Since 1992, Travis has been working in the construction and development industry. He has worked as a Design-Builder, Planner, Project Manager, Construction Manager and Development Consultant. As a planning consultant, he has written strategic and business plans for clients. However, the United Storehouse International (USI) strategic plan was being written without an "apparent" client. As it turned out, the Church at-large would become the intended client as the Spirit of God leads.

Born from the USI strategic plan initiative, this book was originally intended to provide a venue for distribution of the USI concept in an easy to read format for Church leadership. As the book evolved, it became evident that it would also be suitable for all readers.

Travis believes that it is the Lord's sovereign will and interest for His people to have insight and knowledge that is relevant to the times that we live in and scripturally based. By His sovereign power, God will faithfully support and propel whatever He initiates and leads as He is glorified in the process. Therefore, Travis is compelled to commit the United Storehouse International project "primarily" to serving the body of Christ and "secondarily" to those who are in need as directed by Christ. In other words, this is more of an in-reach project to support the church than an outreach function to reach the lost.

WORDS OF INSTRUCTION FROM THE LORD

I was in prayer on one particular occasion, asking God to guide me on matters pertaining to the formation of the United Storehouse International project. I received what seemed to be a random scripture in my mind, Deuteronomy 11:10.

Pertinent points that I derived from this scripture included:

- The task at hand is not to be approached in a typical "bottom-up" manner but rather from a "top-down" mountain top perspective.
- The fuel of this endeavor shall be provided "directly" from God and shall not be subject to conventional means.
- This endeavor involves sewing seed in ways that are well-suited for blessings from God based on His goodness rather than relying on market trends.
- If I am obedient and faithful as God leads me and I continue to serve Him, He will pour out His Spirit upon this endeavor.
- As a result, many will be blessed
- I must be careful not to be drawn away from the task in pursuit of worldly advancement in lieu of God's sovereign will for me or He will turn away from this project and all progress will cease.

[Deuteronomy 11:10-17]

When I read this passage of scripture, it immediately spoke to me in a personal way. From my years of experience in the construction and real estate development industry, I was entertaining the premise of making this project into an offering available to private developers and venture capitalist. I believe the principle is sound enough for presentation to the general public as a lifestyle membership association. For the sake of being thorough and prudent, I have always been a proponent of having exit strategies and contingency plans in the event that the initial target is not reached.

I had been contemplating making this project more "universal" in its application. I believe the Lord sent me to this particular passage in the scriptures to "specifically" instruct me not to be discouraged or swayed by the general market and what it may indicate regarding the "marketability" and degree of "profitability" from this concept. I realized that God's plans don't necessarily utilize exit strategies in the conventional sense. We may fail and receive God's mercy and grace, but we don't get to re-write the script to fit our shortcomings and personal inclinations. In fact, God's Word clearly indicates that His primary exit strategy for those who are called for His purpose is through transitioning the faithful into eternity with Him.

WHAT'S NEXT

This book, **Revival of the Seven**, is a re-introduction to the "modern application" of this 2,000 year old concept started by the Apostolic Church. It is the first of three companion books.

1. REVIVAL OF THE SEVEN
2. HOUSEHOLD FINANCES IN AMERICA – CHRISTIAN ECONOMICS
3. THE MODERN CHURCH – WITHIN WALLS

These (3) books explore topics related to the USI program in detail. Other publications shall be made available as he is led by the Lord to share. In the meantime, Travis plans to spend time promoting the unified Christian culture concept through meeting with Church leaders, gathering more information about Churches around the world and seeking to build partnerships with various Church Organizations. He seeks to provide guidance and counsel to those that feel led and are ready to join in the journey towards utilizing the USI Church development concepts in their local community.

UNITED STOREHOUSE INTERNATIONAL

REFERENCES

(Fair Use Copyright Standards Apply)

INFORMATION & QUOTES

1. Inspiration: The Holy Bible
2. Resources:
    a. Quote: Thomas Jefferson pg. 98
    b. Various Independent Sources

GRAPHICS

1. Created By: Travis E. Hills, Sr.
2. Resources:
    a. Government Symbols & Currency
    b. Public Icons

[page left blank]

Made in United States
Troutdale, OR
11/03/2026

56847392R00121